D1470485

STRANGE BUT TRUE
TENNESSEE

SWEETWATER
PRESS

Strange But True Tennessee

Copyright © 2006 Sweetwater Press

Produced by Cliff Road Books

ISBN-13: 978-1-58173-510-9
ISBN-10: 1-58173-510-3

Design by Miles G. Parsons
Map of Tennessee by Tim Rocks

Printed in The United States of America

STRANGE BUT TRUE TENNESSEE

LYNNE L. HALL

SWEETWATER
PRESS

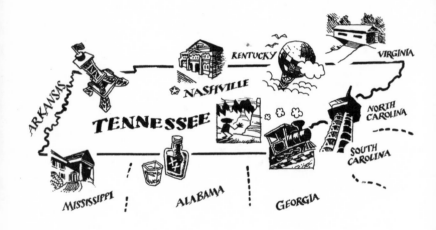

Table of Contents

In a Strange State:

Road Trip Through Strange But True Tennesee

Got a bit of the ham in you? You'll be right at home in Tennessee, where the tourism department has "set the stage for you." Visit their state and they promise to entertain you with their rich musical history. Read their brochures, watch their slick commercials, and you'll be regaled by the scenic beauty of their stage backdrop.

Tennessee, known as the Volunteer State for its willingness to help in a crisis, is marked by the contrasts between its southern roots and cosmopolitan present. You can stroll down shady lanes past magnificent antebellum homes. That is, after you've sat for hours in Nashville's legendarily gridlocked traffic!

Contrasting geography and geology are the state's feature presentations, with the state split into three separate "Grand Divisions." In the East, you'll thrill to the hazy beauty of the Great Smoky Mountains, which take a breathtaking drop into the green vastness of the Tennessee Valley. The rocky terrain of this area was the inspiration for the University of Tennessee anthem, "Rocky Top." You'll find yourself mesmerized by the bustle of Chattanooga, with its world-class aquarium, sophisticated art centers, and exciting outdoor sports attractions.

In a Strange State

There are stars all over Middle Tennessee. The stars of the rolling pasturelands are without a doubt the gleaming, prancing Tennessee Walking Horses, which were born and bred here. Their distinctive rocking-chair gait is both beautiful and exciting to watch. If gorgeous horseflesh doesn't do it for you, don't despair. There's plenty of slick entertainment to be had in Tennessee's own Music City—Nashville—where you can stare agog at the brilliant country stars shooting past.

In West Tennessee, the bucolic serenity gives way to the hustle and bustle of busy Memphis, home of the state's most famous tourist attraction, Graceland. And Nashville's got nuttin' on Memphis, where you can beat your feet down Beale Street, home of the blues and birthplace of rock n' roll.

That's the tourism department's Tennessee—beautiful, elegant, and stately.

Ah, but we've got a different state in mind. Beneath all that beauty and elegance lies a whole other state, and it's a state of pure wackiness, a state filled with quirky characters, extraordinary happenings, weird and spooky places, and some of the most bizarre landmarks ever built. So drop that colorful tourism brochure. Turn off the pretty commercials. Come ham it up in our strange but true presentation!

Strange Statues

We've Got Statues

Scattered willy-nilly across Strange But True Tennessee is an eclectic collection of strange and quirky monuments. You'll find a whole crew of Muffler Men and their snacks—really big burgers and fries—giant cows, and, oh my, a collection of statues in the all together.

ATHENA • NASHVILLE

She's a tall drink of water. Really, really tall. Nashville's statue of Athena, the Greek goddess of wisdom, stands forty-one feet, ten inches. The twelve-ton sculpture is the tallest indoor sculpture in the western world. She's also a shining example, having recently been gilded with sixty-five thousand sheets of twenty-three karat gold. She's quite a sight.

The statue is a replica of the Athena that graced the Parthenon of ancient Greece. Pheidias, reputed to be the greatest sculptor of classical antiquity, sculpted the original. Though an outline of the statue's base is all that remains, we know of its existence because of a detailed description in the building accounts of the Parthenon.

Unveiled in 438 or 437 BC, the statue held a six-foot, four-inch figure of Nike, goddess of victory, in her right hand. Her lance rested on her left shoulder and her left hand supported her shield, which sheltered a snake, symbol of renewal. Eleven other snakes appeared on the statue: two on her belt, two on her wrists, and seven on her breastplate.

With skin of ivory, Athena wore a flowing gold dress. On her head was an intricately detailed helmet, with a sphinx at the apex and a Pegasus, the flying horse, on each side. Other surfaces were just as richly decorated. The shield was carved with scenes from the battle of the Greeks and the Amazons. Athena's breastplate was decorated with snakes and the head of Medusa, and her sandals depicted scenes of the Battle of the Lapiths and the Centaurs. The base on which she stood displayed the birth of Pandora, the first woman born in Greek mythology.

Local artist Alan LeQuire sculpted Nashville's Athena between 1982 and 1990. A full-scale replica, she is constructed of gypsum cement, with skin painted to resemble ivory. Her dress, helmet, shield, the Nike in her right hand, and the Pandora fresco on her base all glitter with gold. She is the centerpiece of Nashville's full-scale replica of the Parthenon, which was built in the 1920s and serves as the city's art museum.

Located in Centennial Park.

BASKETBALL • KNOXVILLE

There's a giant basketball outside the Women's Basketball Hall of Fame. The basketball is thirty feet high and weighs ten tons.

Located at 700 Hall of Fame Drive.

CATFISH • PARIS

It looks fishy to us. Paris is home to the World's Biggest Fish Fry. Maybe that's why they have a statue of a giant catfish flipping its tail at the four-way stop on Highway 70 and Mineral Wells Avenue.

COKE CANS • CLEVELAND

If the Jolly Green Giant's got a thirst, he can hie on over to Cleveland, where he'll find a couple of giant cans of the real thing. The storage tanks at a local bottling plant may just be the world's largest coke cans.

Located on US 64.

EIFFEL TOWER • PARIS

You were expecting the Leaning Tower, perhaps? Really, what attraction is more fittin' for a town named Paris? It is trés apropos. But, hey, check out Old Glory up there on the top! Bet you won't find that on that there Frenchie tower.

Paris, Tennessee's Eiffel Tower is a sixty-foot scale model of France's tower, which is 986 feet tall. The

Paris, Tennessee commemorates the American-French bond with a scaled-down replica of the Eiffel tower. Courtesy of Paris Chamber of Commerce.

brain child of Christian Brothers University (Memphis) engineering professors, the Tennessee tower is constructed of five hundred pieces of Douglas fir and six thousand steel rods. Students, faculty, and alumni from CBU originally assembled it in ten thousand hours.

Assembly, however, posed a dilemma. What to do with it? Hey! Look! There's a Paris, Tennessee! Let's give it to them! And, so, the Eiffel Tower was disassembled, placed on a trailer, and trucked on over to Paris, where it was then reassembled in the town's Memorial Park.

Paris, Tennessee, town fathers see the tower as a symbol of the Franco-American bond in the fight for liberty. They remind folks—who, in light of present circumstances, might wonder— the bond was forged by the Marquis de Lafayette, who brought his own ship and joined George Washington's staff as an unpaid volunteer in the American Revolution. Indeed, the town, which was founded in 1823, was named in honor of the good Marquis. In addition, they speculate that our success in our fight for liberty sparked the French Revolution.

There may be other cities named Paris. And some of those may have their own Eiffel Towers. But none of those towers are taller than this one. It makes a cool attraction. Viva la Paris…Tennessee, y'all!

Located on Volunteer Drive.

NATHAN BEDFORD FORREST • NASHVILLE

The statue of Confederate General Nathan Bedford Forrest astride a rearing steed was erected on a strip of private land near Interstate 65 by a wealthy Nashville attorney in a snit over a zoning rejection. Surrounded by a ring of Confederate flags, the statue is allegedly meant to honor Forrest.

At first glance, that's not so unusual. Forrest joined the Confederate army as a private and rose quickly to the rank of general. He was one of the most innovative and successful Confederate generals, and his tactics in guerrilla warfare are still studied today.

His success on the battlefield notwithstanding, most would agree Forrest is not the best subject to honor, unless, of course, your goal is to stir up controversy. The first whiff of said controversy arose in the Battle of Fort Pillow, where it's alleged that Forrest massacred hundreds of African-American Union soldiers.

His public relations problem was compounded by the fact that after the war, he was a founding member of the Ku Klux Klan and served as its first Grand Wizard. Forrest insisted, however, that the Klan did not consider African-Americans (not the term he used) as the enemy, but rather the carpetbaggers (Yankees that came to the South after the war to take advantage of impoverished Southerners) and scalawags, the term for white Southern Republicans. It's reported that he distanced himself from the organization because of increasing violence.

No doubt, Forrest would not be flattered by this most recent tribute, which is made entirely of fiberglass. The rearing horse is gold-leafed and Forrest is silver-leafed. Horse and rider are connected via a steel rod that emerges from the horse's back and enters Forrest where, well, where he sits. That may explain the wild-eyed, truly frightening look on the good general's face. The statue and the ring of Confederate flags have stirred the expected controversy, with many vehemently objecting to the makeshift park and just as many adamantly defending it as an expression of free speech. We just think it's a sight to see on our Strange But True Tour.

Located off I-65 North between the Old Hickory Boulevard and Harding Road exits.

> Tennessee was divided in its loyalties during the Civil War. When the state seceded to join the Confederacy, East Tennessee tried unsuccessfully to leave the state and stay with the Union. Tennessee contributed one hundred thousand soldiers to the Confederacy, but also contributed fifty thousand to the Union.

GIANT FOOD • KINGSPORT

When the Jolly Green Giant needs a little something to go with that Co-Cola, he'll find plenty to eat around Kingsport. The eighteen Tennessee

Pal's offers fast food in giant portions.
Courtesy of Pal's Sudden Service.

locations of Pal's Sudden Service, an award-winning fast-food joint, are festooned with giant-sized menu items—hamburgers, hot dogs, fries, and drinks. We can just see all that jolly green blood clotting in those giant arteries now!

Located at 1120 East Stone Drive.

ALEX HALEY • KNOXVILLE

There's a twelve-foot statue of Pulitzer Prize winner Alex Haley in Knoxville. Internationally renowned sculptor Tina Allen sculpted the statue of Haley, who is best known for his book and the movie *Roots*. Said to be the largest statue of an African-American in the country, it depicts Haley seated and dressed in a casual sweater. He's gazing out into the Smoky Mountains.

If it truly is the largest African-American statue in the country, it has a long way to go to beat the largest white man statue and the largest Native American. The sixty-seven-foot statue of Sam Houston in Huntsville, Texas, takes the white man prize, followed by the sixty-two-foot statue of a Native American in Skowhegan, Maine.

Haley's statue is located at 1600 Dandridge Avenue.

ANDREW JACKSON • NASHVILLE

Nashville's bronze Equestrian Statue of Andrew Jackson is one of three cast between 1853 and 1880. The other two reside in Washington, D.C. and New Orleans. The statues depict Jackson, aka "Old Hickory," sitting astride a rearing steed and waving his tricorn. They are unique in that sculptor Clark Mills created the statues to be supported only by the two back legs of the rearing horse.

Strange Statues

A gift to the state from the Tennessee Historical Society, the statue in Nashville was unveiled on May 20, 1880, as part of Nashville's centennial celebration. It now stands on the east side of the Tennessee State Capitol.

ANDREW JOHNSON • NASHVILLE

No, we're not repeating ourselves—this is Andrew Johnson, the seventeenth U.S. President. His statue stands at the State Capitol, near the other Andrew president.

Johnson came to Tennessee in 1826 as an uneducated man hoping to make a living as a tailor in the small town of Greenville. He opened a shop in a tiny 13 x 20-foot log cabin, but it wasn't long before his superior oratory skills gained him notice. He began a steady political climb, serving as state senator, U.S. congressman, Tennessee governor, U.S. senator, and U.S. vice president. And he wasn't through yet. As vice president to Abraham Lincoln, he took over the presidency when Lincoln was assassinated, though he did not receive his party's nomination for reelection.

A statue of Andrew Johnson, the seventeenth President of the Unites States, stands at the Capitol in Nashville. Courtesy of the University of Tennessee.

Johnson's tenure as president was turbulent, coming at a time when the country was beginning to heal from the Civil War. He had gained much resentment from Southerners for his decision to remain loyal to the Union when Tennessee seceded. During his presidency, the Thirteenth Amendment abolishing slavery and the Fourteenth Amendment providing equal treatment for all citizens were added to the Constitution. But many, even those in his own party, resented some of his actions. When Johnson attempted to dismiss Edwin Stanton, Lincoln's Secretary of War, Congress impeached him, claiming he had violated a statute prohibiting him from dismissing elected officials without Congressional approval. He was not convicted, but was the first president to be impeached.

After not receiving his party's re-nomination, Johnson returned to Greenville, remaining active in politics until his death in 1875.

Mayfield Dairy Cow • Athens

If you're an ice cream lover, no doubt you're familiar with Mayfield Dairy, maker of that delectably delightful concoction, Moose Tracks. If you're not familiar with the company, fear not. Mayfield is on its way to your city with its mascot, a bodaciously buxom bovine who travels by trailer to spread word of the company's sweet products. The big cow stands about eight feet tall, and when she's not traveling, she stands outside the dairy's headquarters in Athens.

Located at 211 Water Country Parkway.

Strange Statues

MUFFLER MEN OF TENNESSEE

What is this obsession with muffler men? Maybe it's the square jaw. Maybe it's that he's just so darn tall. Whatever the draw, there are a few to be seen in Tennessee.

Chattanooga's muffler man hides inside the Sir Goony Golf course, where, reincarnated as a member of a NASCAR Pit Crew, he holds a tire in one hand and a wrench in the other.

Cross Plains also has a muffler man. He stands guard over the Red River Antique Mall. He may not be the most interesting item, however. He's standing next to a pink elephant.

Kingsport has at least two muffler men. One guards the big food at Pal's Sudden Service. He's been there since 1962, and he's holding a very big burger, with fries and a drink nearby. Another muffler man of sorts has stood at a local barbecue restaurant for more than twenty years. He's a big Native American. Dressed in a loincloth, he stands in front of Pratt's Barn restaurant. Legend has it that several years ago the good people of Kingsport were scandalized when a tornado ripped through town and ripped off the big guy's loincloth. Seems he and Ken have a lot in common. They're not anatomically correct! Well, the loincloth was replaced and, dignity regained, he returned to welcoming folks into the restaurant.

The Munford muffler man is a transient. Seems he just shows up around Christmas time and on the Fourth of July. His job is to help bring customers in to the fireworks stand. He's located on Highway 51 at the Shelby County/Tipton County line.

DOLLY PARTON • SEVIERVILLE

Sevierville has erected a statue of its favorite, and most famous, daughter, Dolly Parton. The statue, located in front of the courthouse, depicts a young Dolly—sans wig and that famous "pair." Sitting atop a rock, she's barefoot, wearing pedal pushers (Remember those? They were the 1960s version of capris), and clutching a guitar.

A young Dolly perches on a rock outside of the Sevierville courthouse.
Courtesy of Sevierville Chamber of Commerce.

Parton, born into dirt poor poverty, began her musical career at an early age, recording her first records and appearing on the Grand Ole Opry by age thirteen. In addition to performing at such an early age, she was an accomplished songwriter, with songs recorded by such country music greats as Kitty Wells and Hank Williams Sr.

The moment she graduated from high school in 1967, she headed out to Nashville in search of fame and fortune. She found both, landing a gig as "girl singer" on the popular *Porter Wagoner Show*, signing a recording contract with RCA Records, and joining the *Grand Ole Opry*. And she just kept going from there, adding movie star to her list of credits and becoming a lasting icon in the country music industry.

Today, Dolly may be best known for her foray into the theme park business. Dollywood, a country music theme park in Pigeon Forge, is Tennessee's number one attraction and is one of the most popular vacation spots in the South. The park features 130 acres of rides, shows and concerts, and arts and crafts.

Dolly's statue is located at 125 Court Avenue.

PINK ELEPHANT • CROSS PLAINS

Nah, you're not drunk. OK. Maybe you are. But you're not hallucinating. There really is a pink elephant wearing Lyndon Johnson glasses and holding a black martini glass in his trunk. He's there at the Red River Antique Mall. Right next to that really big guy wearing jeans and a red flannel shirt. Did we mention that you're not hallucinating?

Located at 8725 Highway 25.

SANDY THE SANDSTONE STATUE • KNOXVILLE

Sandy the statue is one of the most recognized pieces of ancient Native American art. Carved from a single piece of sandstone, he measures eighteen-inches tall and twelve-inches wide. He's an odd, squatty little man, kneeling on his left knee, with his hands resting on his knees.

Sandy was found at the Sellers Archeological Site in Wilson County in 1939, along with a similar female statue. Dating from the late prehistoric Mississippian period—1200 to 1400 AD—

the statues are thought to represent an important ancestor or founder of a family lineage.

Sandy, an international traveler, has become the logo for the University of Tennessee's Frank H. McClung Museum. You can view him, his female companion, and a whole host of other important exhibits there.

Located at 1327 Circle Park Drive.

WAR DOG MEMORIAL • KNOXVILLE

Oohhh! It's a puppy. Oh, OK. So it's a big puppy. This remarkably lifelike statue of a Doberman Pincher is a heartwarming tribute to the hundreds of war dogs that served in the Marine Corps in World War II. Most of these four-legged heroes were Dobermans, but German Shepherds, Labrador Retrievers, and a Collie or two also served. Their official job title was sentry, messenger, or scout, but their true service was that as devoted friend to their Marine companions.

Dr. Maurice Acree's love for

The War Dog statue commemorates the canines
that lost their lives during WWII.
Courtesy of Chad Huguenin.

Strange Statues

Doberman Pinschers spurred the donation of the memorial, an exact replica of the official memorial in Guam, to the University of Tennessee College of Veterinary Medicine. It not only honors war dogs, but also serves as a tribute to the special bond between dog and man.

Located in front of the College of Veterinary Medicine.

Natural and Manmade Wonders

Wackiness abounds on the byways of our Strange But True Tennessee. No sappy theme parks here. Instead there's a weird hodgepodge of natural and manmade wonders.

APPALACHIAN CAVERNS

It's one of the most historically active caverns in the country. In the past, it's served as a gathering place for Native Americans, a graveyard, a Confederate hospital, a source for guano, a garbage dump, and a tourist attraction.

And that's just in the last few hundred years. Archeological evidence shows that activity in the fifty-million-year-old cave dates back to prehistoric times. Treasures found within the cave include a mastodon tooth and the bones of an extinct horse that were found by a local archeologist and paleontologist.

As a meeting place for Native Americans, it's rumored that tribal members are buried there, though no effort has been made toward verification. There has been confimation, however, of the story of John Linville, a nineteenth century trapper who was killed by Indians and was buried in the cave by his brother, Jim. Planning to find a proper burial spot, Jim returned a few years later only to discover that his brother's remains had mysteriously disappeared—reportedly dug up and disbursed by

Natural and Manmade Wonders

Indians. The account is verified by Jim's diary, which bears out the details. The gravesite, which lies in the area called the Passage of Time, was filled in by the cave's owner. The cave's Lineville Creek is named for the brothers.

One-hour guided tours traverse almost a mile of walkways and take you through the cool interior of the cave. An elaborate lighting system illuminates the rich colors provided by manganese, iron, calcium, and copper.

For the adventurous, wild tours are available. These tours last three-and-a-half hours and wind through the undeveloped sections of the cave.

Gifts and souvenirs are available in the gift shop, which also features a display of artifacts found on the property.

Located at 420 Cave Hill Road.

BUCK BALD • COKER CREEK

On a clear day you can see...North Carolina! Buck Bald is truly one of Tennessee's purple mountain majesties, with a breathtaking panoramic view of three states. It's called "bald" because its summit is treeless.

Scientific explanations abound for the bald mountains— primeval upheaval, erosion, a stratigraphically lower layer of schist. We like the Cherokee version better.

It says the bald mountains exist because a horrible, sharp-clawed winged beast once lived on the mountaintop. This terrible, hungry beast would kidnap and eat little Native American children. The Cherokee cleared the forest from the mountain summit and captured the beast. They then prayed to the Great Spirit, who killed the beast and from there on out kept the mountaintop clear of trees.

The mountain is festooned with hiking and biking trails, one of which is a six-mile climb to the top, where you'll find a breathtaking view.

Buck Bald mountain gets its name from its treeless peak.
Photo by Leslie Copeland–Wells, Coker Creek, TN.

Don't expect to breathe again, though, until you reach the Hiawassee River at the bottom. For what goes up must come down, and the six-mile downhill run is awesome.

Located on Highway 68.

CRAIGHEAD CAVERNS • SWEETWATER

Craighead Caverns is an extensive cave system with an intriguing history and a number of mysterious natural wonders. Without a doubt, the most mystifying—and electrifying—of the caverns' marvels is the Lost Sea, also included in our strange attractions. We'll save that tale for later. First, the caverns.

The known history for Craighead Caverns dates back to the Pleistocene Era—some twenty thousand years ago—when an unfortunate prehistoric jaguar wandered in and became lost in the profound darkness of the inner labyrinths. The big kitty's keen night vision must have deserted him, for his tracks weave in and out of the deepest, darkest chambers of the cave. He wandered for days before plunging to his death into a deep crevice. Some of his bones, which were discovered in 1939, are on display in the American

A family discovers history and beauty in Craighead Caverns.
Courtesy of Craighead Caverns.

Museum of Natural History in New York. The remainder of the bones and plaster casts of his paw prints are among the exhibits at the visitor center.

Fast forward. Evidence shows that the caverns were a popular meeting spot for the Cherokee who inhabited Tennessee before the settlers arrived. From a small natural opening on the side of the mountain, the cavern opens into a series of large chambers. Almost a mile inside the cave is the Council Room, so named because of the large number of Native American artifacts found here.

Keep going. When white settlers arrived in the 1800s, they discovered the cave and its constant 58-degree temperature, perfect for refrigeration of perishables, such as potatoes and other vegetables.

During the Civil War, the cave was mined for saltpeter to be used in gunpowder. Legend has it that a Union spy penetrated the guarded cave and almost blew up the mining operation. He was captured just in time and supposedly was executed near a large gum tree that grows at the cave's entrance.

Onward into modern history. In 1915, the cave became Party Central. A dance floor was installed in one of the large upper rooms, and cockfights were a favorite pastime. Meanwhile, in other areas of the huge cave system, moonshiners were plying their clandestine trade, brewing up that powerful potion with the kick of a mule.

The rich history of the caverns is fascinating, but it's secondary to the beauty of the natural formations of the cave, which include anthodites. These are delicate, spiny clusters known as "cave flowers." They are rare formations, and their abundance in the caverns led the U.S. Department of the Interior to designate Craighead Caverns as a Registered National Landmark.

The caverns are open every day but Christmas Day and daily tours are offered. There's also a Wild Tour Adventure, which takes visitors through undeveloped areas of the cave. Participants get to really explore the cave system and crawl through cracks, crevices, nooks, and crannies. Overnight cave tours can be booked in advance.

Natural and Manmade Wonders

CRYSTAL SHRINE GROTTO • MEMPHIS

Hidden deep within the confines of Memorial Park Cemetery, down a silent, shady drive, lies the Crystal Shrine Grotto. You'll know it by the single rock spire that rises among the gravestones.

Crystal Shrine Grotto is a crystal cave made of natural quartz, crystal, and semiprecious stones carved from the hillside. Artist Donicio Rodriguez, a descendent of the artistic Aztec nation, carved the cave in the 1930s. Its entrance is through a hole in an enormous tree stump—Abraham's Oak, named for Abraham of the Bible. Don't be fooled though, the tree is not made of wood. Rodriguez, who specialized in creating concrete sculptures that resembled wood and stone, created the trunk.

A sculpture of Jesus' head is one of the many pieces of art found in Crystal Shrine Grotto.
Courtesy of Crystal Shrine Grotto.

Inside the grotto cavern is an illustration of "Christ's Journey on the Earth From Birth To Resurrection," an odd conglomeration of abstract scenes mixed in with traditional religious dioramas. At the entrance, above the guest book, is a plaque of "The Most Beautiful Head in History." We'll give you a hint...his initials are JC.

Located at 5668 Poplar Avenue.

CUMBERLAND CAVERNS • MCMINNVILLE

Cumberland Caverns is Tennessee's largest show cave and is listed as a U.S. National Landmark. The cave, an integration of two caves—Higgenbotham Cave and Henshaw Cave, both discovered in the 1800s—encompasses thirty-two miles of explored area.

During the War of 1812 and the Civil War, nitrates were mined from Henshaw Cave, and gunpowder was manufactured by heating deposits of calcium nitrate and potash in huge vats. Saltpeter crystallized from the liquid and was used in gunpowder. Evidence of this industry can still be found.

Shortly after the Civil War, Higgenbotham Cave was penetrated more than a mile, where a huge avenue sixty feet wide, ten feet high, and two-thousand feet long, now called the Ten Acre Room, was discovered. In 1953, it was discovered that the two caves were separated only by a breakdown in a chamber adjacent to the Ten Acre Room. Opening this breakdown connected the two caves and facilitated the exploration of a whole new series of galleries, called The Great Extension.

Visitors admire a stalagmite at Cumberland Caverns.
Courtesy of Cumberland Caverns.

Natural and Manmade Wonders

Cumberland Caverns contains some of the largest subterranean rooms and spectacular formations in the eastern United States. There are waterfalls, sparkling pools, and even a seventeen-hundred pound chandelier. The cave's most celebrated feature is the Monument Pillar, a fifteen-foot-high gleaming white stalagmite, with a green pool at its base and sparkling calcite crystals embedded within its surface. It's internationally known. Daily tours, offered from May 1 until October 31, include the historic 1812 saltpeter mine and God of the Mountain, an original underground pageant of light and sound.

And, oh! Are ya looking for some place really different for that special occasion? Look no further! At Cumberland Caverns you can rent the grand Underground Ballroom, which seats four hundred.

Located at 1437 Cumberland Caverns Road.

DOE RIVER COVERED BRIDGE • ELIZABETHTON

Here's a bit of trivia for you. Got any idea why there are covered bridges? Thought so. Well, it's because back in the day when wood was the only construction material available and bridges were terribly expensive to build and maintain, they were covered to protect their critical load-bearing components. So, now ya know.

The Doe River Covered Bridge, built in 1882 for the exorbitant sum of $3,000, stretches 134 feet across the Doe River. It's constructed of plain oak boards fastened together with hand-forged nails and threaded spikes. One of the oldest covered bridges in the state, it was still in use until just a few years ago.

The bridge is included in the National Registry of Historic Sites and is the most photographed landmark in Carter County. Bring your camera and a lunch to picnic in the adjacent park.

Built in 1882, the Doe River Covered Bridge is one of the oldest covered bridges in the state.
Courtesy of Elizabethton Chamber of Commerce.

Located off Highway 19 East.

EBBING AND FLOWING SPRING • ROGERSVILLE

This stream is a world-renown phenomenon. It's one of only two springs on Earth that ebbs and flows just like the ocean tides. Scientists and researchers from all over the world have studied it.

It's not gonna be one of your more fast-paced attractions, however. The spring ebbs and flows on a two-hour and forty minute schedule. Guess you could sit and twiddle your thumbs while you wait. Or you could check out historic Rogersville, home to the oldest post office, inn, and courthouse in Tennessee.

Natural and Manmade Wonders

ELEPHANT SANCTUARY • HOHENWALD

Where do elephants go to retire? If they're lucky they end up at the Elephant Sanctuary, the nation's first and largest natural habitat developed for endangered African and Asian elephants.

Founded in 1995, the sanctuary operates on twenty-seven hundred acres of green pastures, old-growth forests, and spring-fed ponds. It has two distinct missions. The first, and most important, is to provide refuge to old or sick elephants retired from circuses and zoos. The second is to educate the public about the crisis facing these endangered creatures.

Although the sanctuary is closed to the general public, patron donors are invited to visit and learn about these playful, complex, and highly intelligent animals.

FLYING SAUCER HOUSE • CHATTANOOGA

The aliens have landed! And they're living on Signal Mountain! And they look just like a couple of elderly humans! Chattanooga's Flying Saucer House was built as a lark by Tennessee native Curtis King and his sons in the 1970s. It looks just like something out of a 1950s B movie—saucer shaped with

The Flying Saucer House is a residential home in Chattanooga.
Courtesy of Chattanooga CVB.

porthole windows all around and resting on six legs. Entrance into the house is made through a stairway protruding from underneath.

Located on Signal Mountain Road.

FORBIDDEN CAVERNS • SEVIERVILLE

The Forbidden Caverns has a storied history, from the Eastern Woodland Indians, who used it as shelter in the winter, to the legend of the Indian princess who was lost in a "forbidden" cavern, to its twenty-year incarnation as a moonshine factory from the 1920s until 1943. Forbidden Caverns has all the requisite cavern accouterments—towering natural chimneys, spectacular formations, a crystal clear stream, and numerous grottos. Besides all that, the cavern boasts one of the largest walls of rare cave onyx known to exist!

Forbidden Caverns is open from April 1 through November 30. There are daily tours that take you through the caverns and tell you of the Indian legends and the Moonshine Days, with a tour of the actual moonshine still.

The Forbidden Caverns is located at 455 Blowing Cave Road.

FROZEN HEAD STATE NATURAL AREA • WARTBURG

This beautiful area is located in the Cumberland Mountains of Eastern Tennessee. With an elevation of 3,324 feet it is one of the highest peaks west of the Great Smoky Mountains. From the observation tower at the top, you can see Cumberland Plateau, Tennessee Ridge and Tennessee Valley, and the Great Smoky Mountains.

Natural and Manmade Wonders

The high elevation is the reason for the unusual name. In winter months, the mountain peaks are capped with snow and ice while the lower areas remain clear, thus giving rise to the "Frozen Head" name.

Located at 964 Flat Fork Road.

GEOGRAPHIC CENTER OF TENNESSEE • MURFREESBORO

Say you like being in the middle of things? Well, come to Murfreesboro, where you'll be center stage. The geographic center of Tennessee is located on Old Lascassas Pike, just a half-mile from the campus of Middle Tennessee State University. A stone obelisk marks the spot.

Located in Old Lascassas Park.

GRACELAND • MEMPHIS

Unless you've lived the last thirty years on another planet, you know all about the life of the King of Rock and Roll. You know about his humble beginnings in Tupelo, Mississippi; about the move to Nashville, Tennessee, where he first rocked the world with his new brand of music, a blend of blues and rockabilly; about his rise as a movie star; about his later years, of poor health issues and his tragic death thirty years ago. So, we won't bore you with all that.

We will let you in on a little secret, though. We're fans. Yep, we can admit it. We still get a little flutter when we see that trademark sneer on late night movies. We still get a bit of a thrill when we hear that golden voice. No doubt about it, the boy had some charisma.

Still, we're at a loss to explain the phenomenon that is ELVIS, and the millions of fans who just can't let him go. Some of these folks make yearly pilgrimages to pay homage to him at Graceland.

On their pilgrimages, they wander through the rooms of Graceland, marveling at the stained glass framing the living room; the mother's room done completely in royal purple; the profusion of greenery, furry furniture, green shag carpeting, and monkey sculptures of the jungle room. They tour the trophy building in opened-mouthed awe at the gold records on the wall, the awards, the jewelry, and the

About 600,000 tourists come to see Elvis's home annually.
©ELVIS PRESLEY ENTERPRISES, INC.

stage costumes. They conclude their tour in solemnity with a stroll through the Meditation Garden, where Elvis, his parents, and his grandmother are laid to rest.

More than six-hundred thousand people visit Graceland yearly. A couple of tips for your trip: carefully consider whether you want to visit on January 9 or August 16, since they are, no doubt, the busiest days. January 8 (1935) is Elvis's birthday and August 16 (1977) is his date of death.

Natural and Manmade Wonders

Oh! But when you do visit…make plans to stay at the official Heartbreak Hotel, located adjacent to Graceland. The rooms and suites of this 128-room full-service hotel reflect the "personal style for which the King of Rock 'n Roll was famous." No doubt about it, the King had an eclectic sense of style.

Graceland is located at 3734 Elvis Presley Boulevard. For more information on Graceland and the Heartbreak Hotel visit www.elvis.com.

GREAT SMOKY MOUNTAINS NATIONAL PARK • TENNESSEE

Talk about your purple mountain majesties! Imagine trekking through untamed forests as pristine as the day the early settlers first stepped foot in them. As you hike, you'll pass wild rivers that snake down the mountains, churning up white water rapids and delighting with sparkling waterfalls.

Keep your eyes and your ears open, for wild things live here. Because of the park's unique northeast-to-southwest orientation, which kept glaciers from invading the mountains during the last ice age, a huge diversity of plant and animal life migrated here. More than one hundred thousand species have been documented, and scientists believe that another ninety thousand may also live here. No other place of comparable size can match the diversity. So walk softly and carry a big camera.

That camera will come in handy for those gorgeous landscape shots, too. The scenic beauty of the Smokies is unmatched anywhere. Especially if you're lucky enough to visit in the fall, when the mountainsides are ablaze with the brilliant colors of autumn. But don't despair if summer is your season, for during those warm months, the mountains are riotously splendiferous with carpets of wildflowers and forests of blooming trees.

Don't think that one trip will do it for the Smokies. There are more than eight hundred miles of hiking trails in the Great Smoky Mountains National Park. There are also lots more things

No matter what the season, the landscape of the Great Smokey Mountains is awe-inspiring.
Courtesy of the National Park Service.

to do, such as picnicking, horseback riding, fishing, biking, camping, backpacking, bird watching, sightseeing, and auto touring. Whew! Better stock up on energy bars, 'cause you're not gonna wanna miss a thing!

The Great Smoky Mountains National Park was named for the smoky bluish haze that often enwraps the mountains.

Natural and Manmade Wonders

Hundred Oaks Castle • Winchester

No, you haven't been teleported over to merry old England. There really is a castle standing there in front of you. Called Hundred Oaks Castle, for the number of oak trees on the property, it began life as a normal two-story Southern plantation home, originally built in 1830.

Things went awry when owner Arthur Marks was given a diplomatic position in England. He was quite taken with the architecture of the ancient castles, and with Mary Hunt, a wealthy Nashville native he met there. The two were married in Scotland and returned to Winchester in 1889, at which time Marks began converting his plantation home into Hundred Oaks Castle.

The house was converted into a twelve-bedroom castle, with a forty-foot high ceiling in the Great Hall, a dining room with oak beamed ceilings, and a study patterned after Sir Walter's study in Scotland. There are towers, a carriage house, underground tunnels, and beautiful gardens. The stones for the castle were transported by wagon from Sewannee Mountain, the brick was baked in Winchester, and the woodwork was hand carved by a local craftsman.

After Marks died of typhoid fever, Mary remarried and the castle changed hands numerous times. It was bought in 1900 by an order of Roman Catholic Priests, who converted the library into a chapel complete with stained glass windows, which were promptly removed when the property was again sold.

Through the next decades, the property changed hands numerous times. In 1990, a fire destroyed one wing of the castle and it remained boarded up until 1996. That's when the Kent Bramlett Foundation, a charitable organization founded by P.K. and Shirley Bramlett in honor of their son who was killed in a car wreck, purchased it. The Bramletts have begun to renovate the castle, furnishing two suites in the castle's attic as a sanctuary for those who need a quiet place to mourn lost loved ones.

The Castle is open for tours, luncheons, and special occasions by appointment.

INCLINE RAILROAD • CHATTANOOGA

It's been called America's Most Amazing Mile and no wonder. As the World's Steepest Passenger Incline, Tennessee's Incline Railroad climb's the steepest—and most scenic—part of Lookout Mountain.

During the mid-1800s, most of Lookout Mountain was owned by two families. The Whitesides owned most of the mountain in Tennessee—having bought it at auction for 1 cent per acre. The Cravens owned the property on the northern section of the mountain and built a home there that still bears this name.

Colonel Whitesides, a savvy businessman, built a toll road up the mountain, charging an exorbitant $2 per toll. When the yellow fever epidemic hit Chattanooga, thousands fled the city to Lookout Mountain, which was known for its healthful climate. They later complained about paying the high toll, and, in response, the St. Elmo Turnpike was built.

To make up for lost revenues, Whitesides began charging for access to The Point, the observation point of the spectacular views that was the destination of many visitors. The fee angered visitors, many of whom refused to pay and some of whom forced their way to The Point. Whitesides then erected a fence and hired armed guards to stand watch. He also contracted with a livery service to take passengers up The Point, preventing anyone not riding with that livery from visiting there. This action angered competing livery owners

Incline Railroad is the world's steepest passenger incline.
Courtesy of Chattanooga CVB.

and others with an interest in Lookout Mountain.

As a result, a group of investors built a hotel off the edge of the mountain just below The Point. They planned a tower that would extend to the level of The Point and provide patrons with the same view. To transport building supplies and customers, they also built a small incline railroad Incline #1, which ran up the mountain to just below The Point. The hotel—The Point Hotel—served as the Incline station.

The Point Hotel opened in 1888, with four stories and fifty-eight rooms. To solve the dilemma of getting customers to the top of the mountain to view the attractions, the investors built the Narrow Gauge Railroad, which ran an end run around Whitesides's property, ending at Natural Bridge, one of the most popular tourist attractions.

By the late 1880s, Lookout Mountain had become a popular tourist attraction as well, and competing investors built a Broad Gauge Railroad that also ran a circuitous route up the mountain. Finally, Whitesides, who seems to have learned his lesson about high prices, built Incline #2, the current Incline Railroad. His railroad was the fastest and most economical way up the mountain, and within two years, the other two railroads were out of business.

The Incline Railroad opened in 1895, climbing the steepest part of Lookout Mountain. A technical marvel, it claims a 72.7 percent incline, the steepest in the world. The original cars were made of wood and powered by coal-burning steam engines. In 1911, electric power was introduced.

Today, two one-hundred-horsepower engines power the Incline Railroad. It chugs up the mile from the base to the summit in a scenic thirty-minute trip, attracting tourists from around the world. The adventure begins at historic St. Elmo Station, with its large covered porches, steeply pitched roof, and tri-color paint scheme. Here, you'll find the Incline Centennial Exhibits, a rare photographic history of the Incline Railroad and Lookout Mountain.

You'll disembark at Lookout Mountain Station, where you

can indulge your sweet tooth at the Candy Connection, buy cheesy souvenirs at the gift shop, and get a break from the screaming kids when you send them to the Mile High Arcade.

Leaving the station, you can take your pick of attractions, including Ruby Falls, Rock City, and the Natural Bridge. The Point is now a part of The Point Park, which commemorates the Civil War Battle of Lookout Mountain. Included within the park is the Cravens house, which played a pivotal role in the battle. There are hiking trails that offer a glimpse at the breathtaking scenery and abundant wildlife.

Board the Incline Railroad at 3917 St. Elmo Avenue.

THE LOST SEA • SWEETWATER

The Lost Sea is a remarkable body of water located deep within Craighead Caverns. It was discovered in 1905, when a thirteen-year-old boy squirmed his way through a small opening three hundred feet underground and found himself in a colossal chamber half filled with water. The room was so large that its darkness swallowed the beam of light from his small flashlight, revealing neither ceiling nor far wall. The boy often talked of hurling mud balls as far as he could, hearing only splashes in all directions.

Divers with every manner of modern equipment have explored the Lost Sea without reaching its full extent. The lake's visible portion is eight hundred feet long and two hundred and twenty feet wide. Beneath the water lie more wonders. Divers have discovered a series of huge sunken rooms. One brave diver ventured into the rooms with a sonar device. Staying close to a wall so that he could find his way back out, he aimed the device in all directions, only to discover that the room was so vast that the device was unable to take any readings. More than thirteen acres of the lake have been mapped, with no end found.

Visitors marvel at the largest underground lake in the world.
Courtesy of Craighead Caverns.

Daily tours of Craighead Caverns include a glass-bottom boat tour of the Lost Sea, which is stocked with some of the largest Rainbow trout in the country. Forget bringing along that line and pole, though. Fishing is verboten!

The Lost Sea has been designated by the *Guinness Book of World Records* as the largest underground lake in the world. Because of the abundance of the rare anthodite formation found within Craighead Caverns, the Lost Sea also has been designated as a Registered National Landmark.

The Lost Sea is open every day but Christmas Day and daily tours are offered.

Natural and Manmade Wonders

MILLENNIUM MANOR • ALCOA

What if you truly believed you were going to live forever? What kind of house do you think you would build? Maybe you can get a few pointers at the Millennium Manor.

Seems William Nicholson, the manor's builder, was a devout man with a unique translation of the Bible. He believed that "everlasting life" meant that, if your faith was strong enough, you'd live forever. Since he believed his faith was strong enough, Nicholson knew he'd need a house to last the millennia. So, that's what he built.

Drafting his wife, Fair, as his only helper, Nicholson began construction in 1938, at age sixty. After his eight-hour shift at the Alcoa plant just across the road from his chosen home site, the elderly couple toiled six to eight hours into the night, hauling great slabs of Tennessee pink marble from a nearby quarry, some weighing as much as three hundred pounds. Nicholson built a ramp and cart to haul the slabs up to the roof.

Using the same Roman architecture of arches and keystones that survives in buildings two thousand years old, Nicholson built a two-story, fourteen room home that has all the amenities a soul would need for a very, very long and happy life, including a sauna and a dungeon. What more could you ask for?

The home is an architectural marvel, with the stone roof and walls set in the arch and keystone construction. According to experts, this construction method alone might last an eternity. But that didn't satisfy Nicholson. He further reinforced his three thousand foot structure by pouring more than four thousand bags of concrete and allowing the cement to seep into and around the huge slabs of stone. The roof is estimated to weigh 432 tons and is able to withstand the weight of several tanks. The walls and floors are four feet thick, with pipe embedded deep within the walls.

Millennium Manor may well exist forever. Nicholson, however, won't be living there. He died in 1965. In the years since his death, the manor has suffered many indignities, including ten years of being rented out to strangers and, most recently, vandalism by local youths.

Today, however, there has been a reprieve. A Knoxville firefighter now owns Millennium Manor and is restoring it. No doubt he expects a long life there—but not forever!

Located at 500 North Wright Road.

NATCHEZ TRACE PARKWAY • TUPELO

The Natchez Trace Parkway closely parallels the Old Natchez Trace, one of the world's first roadways. The Trace began as a series of primitive paths formed through the wilderness by repeated passage of herds of buffalo and other animals. Later, the Trace was used by various tribes of Native Americans, who used it until the arrival of European explorers and American settlers. Time gradually linked the trails and they began to be used for transportation and trade. For twenty years the Trace was the most significant highway of the Old Southwest and one of the most important highways of the nation.

Natural and Manmade Wonders

The earliest Americans to use the Old Natchez Trace were the flatboat men of the Tennessee and Kentucky river valleys. Known as the "Kaintucks," these mountain settlers would build flatboats, load them with produce and animal pelts, and float them down the Mississippi, Cumberland, and Ohio rivers to Natchez to sell. For the

Natchez Trace Parkway has 444 miles of history and hiking.
Courtesy of the National Park Service.

return trip, the men would break up their flatboats, and head home on foot up the Old Natchez Trace.

The return trip, a 450-mile trek from Natchez to Nashville, took fifteen to twenty days, and was fraught with danger. Robbers and highwaymen, knowing the returning settlers were flush with money from their sales, would lie in wait along the Mississippi Territory section of the Trace. After the settlers were killed, they would be disemboweled. Their stomach cavities would be filled with stones and they would be sunk into the river.

By the 1800s, the Trace was recognized as a vital route, and was extended postal service. Congress ordered the Army to clear the road for the postal route and make improvements. Inns, called "stands," and trading posts began popping up every few miles, and by 1818 more than fifty such establishments dotted the Trace from Natchez to Bear Creek on the Alabama border.

Today, the Natchez Trace Parkway traces 180 segments of the Old Natchez Trace, traversing 444 miles across Mississippi, Alabama, and Tennessee. The Parkway begins in Tennessee, near Franklin, and extends 102 miles, through seven counties. All along the way, you can explore historic sites, such as Indian mounds and archeological sites, exhibits and sites of old "stands," and historic homes.

In addition to these sites, the Parkway has eighty-seven miles of trail for hiking, biking, and horseback riding. The Parkway is one of America's 75 National Scenic Byways and 21 All-American Roads. It's officially designated a National Parkway, a National Forest Scenic Byway, and a National Scenic Byway.

THE PARTHENON • NASHVILLE

It's a mystery why Nashville's city officials decided that a full-scale replica of the Greek Parthenon was the perfect symbol for the city's Centennial Exposition in 1897, but, hey, there it is, standing proudly as the centerpiece of Centennial Park. Seems that the Parthenon was such a big hit at the Centennial celebration that city fathers decided it would make a great tourist attraction. They were right.

The original Parthenon dates back to 438 BC. Its builders did their homework, even orienting it facing east to allow light to enter the building as the sun came up and the doors were opened.

Nashville's bronze doors weigh seven-and-a-half tons each. They are twenty-four feet high, seven feet wide, and one foot thick. There are two sets of these huge doors in both Parthenons—four total. Though closely similar, the Athens doors were wooden with bronze overlay, and so weighed less.

A re-creation of the forty-two foot statue of Athena (see Strange Statues section) is the focus of Nashville's Parthenon, just as it was in antiquity, and the plaster replicas of the Parthenon Marbles are direct casts of the original sculptures.

Your tour of the Parthenon is self-guided, though docents are available to answer questions and fill in details about the history of the building. Guided tours are available with reservations.

THE PEABODY HOTEL • MEMPHIS

The Peabody Hotel first opened in 1869, and since that time it's become known as the South's Grand Hotel. A fourteen story Italian Renaissance landmark, the hotel is luxury punctuated by true Southern hospitality. Marble pillars, hand-painted skylights, and a grand piano that graces the Grand Lobby will have you gawking at the same time you check to make sure your lipstick's not smeared.

Choose between four award-winning restaurants, white linen affairs all, and two bars. Or perhaps you'd like a spot of high tea at Chez Phillippe? Just plan to come off that hip pocket, bubba. This here's a luxury hotel, ya know.

Yeah, yeah, all that's well and good. But the reason most folks visit the Peabody is to watch them ducks march. It's a Peabody tradition. At 11:00 a.m., the elevator door opens, a red carpet is unrolled, and the hotel's five ducks emerge to strains of Sousa's "King Cotton March." With great pomp and circumstance they shilly shally to the lobby's ornate fountain, and hop in, where they spend the day preening, splashing, and generally looking cute. Then at 5:00

Ducks bathe in the fountain at the Peabody Hotel. Courtesy of Memphis CVB.

p.m., it's rewind time. The ducks march back into the elevator and are whisked back up to their luxury digs on the roof.

It all started back in the 1930s, with Peabody General Manager Frank Schutt and a friend returning from a weekend hunting trip. The two good old boys may have had a nip or two of that Tennessee sippin' whiskey, we're not sure, but for some reason they thought it was a good idea to put a few of their live duck decoys into the Peabody fountain. The rest is history.

Located at 149 Union Avenue.

Natural and Manmade Wonders

ROCK CITY • CHATTANOOGA

Rock City is one of the last surviving tourist attractions of a bygone era. Opened in 1932, it's a wonderful example of man's ability to kitsch up Mother Nature and turn the world into a billboard.

Even before the Civil War, the area had earned the name the Rock City, because of the immense boulder formations arranged as though to accommodate streets and lanes. Nearby, a one thousand ton boulder balances atop two points of a small rock base and the view from atop an outcropping called Lover's Leap affords a spectacular view of the 140-foot waterfall. Atop the mountain, you have a bird's-eye view of seven states.

Unique advertising has made Rock City very popular; more than five hundred thousand people visit annually.
Courtesy of Chattanooga CVB.

When Garnet and Frieda Carter came to Lookout Mountain in the 1920s, they took a look at all that natural beauty and thought….hmm…needs a little something. Garnet was the consummate huckster, while Frieda had visions of fairies and gnomes dancing in her head. They bought seven hundred acres, which encompassed the Rock City area, and began construction on Fairyland, a residential neighborhood.

When construction on the planned golf course took much longer than expected, Garnet, in an attempt to appease new residents, quickly built a Lilliputian course, now recognized as the first miniature golf course. The idea proved popular and Garnet began franchising his Tom Thumb golf courses across the nation.

Frieda, meanwhile, still had those visions of fairies and gnomes. What better place to build a fairytale land than Rock City? Setting out a trail that wound through the unique rock formations and ended at Lover's Leap, she collected wildflowers and other plants and transplanted them beside her trail. All along the way, she placed statues of gnomes and famous fairy tale characters that she had imported from Germany. Within a darkened cave, she fashioned Fairyland Caverns and Mother Goose Village, a wonderland of elves and gnomes and fairies and nursery rhyme characters. She covered the walls, floors, and ceilings of each underground room with sparkling crystals and fake stalagmites and stalactites.

Garnet returned from his travels and looked upon what his wife hath wrought. He saw that it was good and said, "Hey, I can sell this!"

Rock City officially opened as a tourist attraction on May 21, 1932. To help draw in the masses and point the way to the mountaintop, Garnet hired Clark Byers, a young painter, to travel around the country, offering to paint farmers' barns for free. Well, almost for free. The catch was they had to agree to let him paint three words on each barn's roof: SEE ROCK CITY.

Byers was an industrious traveler, who for thirty years braved angry bulls, rain storms, and lightening bolts to climb the slippery barn roofs and paint his appointed message. Barns as far north as Michigan and as far west as Texas—and all points in between—soon sported Garnet's billboard. The advertising barns became a slice of true Americana, lining the highways of our youth. But, like our youth, the barns are quickly slipping away from us. Of the nine hundred original barns, only about one hundred remain, some of which have been designated as historic landmarks. As a marketing ploy, the barns were a huge success, drawing tourists in by the thousands. More than five hundred thousand people annually, to be precise.

Come, see the wonders of Lookout Mountain at 1400 Patten Road.

Ruby Falls • Chattanooga

Ruby Falls lies deep within Lookout Mountain Cave. It was first discovered by Leo Lambert, a Tennessee cave enthusiast. Lookout Mountain Cave has been used through the centuries as a campsite for Native Americans, a hideout for outlaws, and a Civil War hospital.

In 1923, Lambert purchased the cave with the idea of developing it as a tourist attraction. In 1928, while digging a shaft for an elevator, he discovered a small opening at 260 feet down. Scrambling through, he explored the cave for seventeen hours and emerged with tales of beautiful formations and best of all, a wondrous, spectacular waterfall.

On his next trip, Lambert brought his wife, Ruby. So, now you know how the falls got its name. Anyway, Lambert built an entrance building modeled after a fifteenth century Irish castle, made from limestone removed from the elevator shaft, and opened the cave to the public.

Ruby Falls is open every day but Christmas, with guided tours conducted daily. There's also the Lookout Mountain observation tower and the Fun Forest Playground to enjoy.

Water plummets 145 feet down Ruby Falls
in Lookout Mountain Cave.
Courtesy of Chattanooga CVB.

Located at 1720 South Scenic Highway.

SPACE NEEDLE • GATLINBURG

Shades of Seattle! Tennessee's Space Needle was opened as a tourist attraction in 1970 as the Smoky Mountains' answer to its counterpart in Seattle. The 342-foot tower contains two elevators to the top—where you can get a 360° bird's eye view of the surrounding scenery.

Located at 115 Historic Nature Trail.

The Sunsphere in Knoxville was built for the 1982 World's Fair.

SUNSPHERE • KNOXVILLE

Knoxville's Sunsphere was the centerpiece of the 1982 World's Fair, held in Knoxville. In keeping with the fair's Energy Turns the World theme, the Sunsphere on its 266-foot tower was called The Tower of Power. The sphere has a volume of 203,689 cubic feet with a surface of 16,742 square feet. Its revolving restaurant accommodated 376 diners and a top level observation deck contained 120 seats.

In the 1970s, Knoxville was a bare place. Seems that in the spring of 1974 more than five thousand Knoxvillans indulged in the national craze of streaking—that is, running through a public place wearin' nuttin' atoll. So many of Knoxville's citizens streaked down Cumberland Avenue in the altogether that year that veteran broadcaster Walter Cronkite named Knoxville The Streaking Capital of the World. Don't look, Ethel!

The fair was such a financial disaster that there has not been another World Fair since. The Sunsphere, however, was a big hit and, though it is now closed, it has become the centerpiece of Knoxville's skyline.

Located at 525 Henley Street.

TENNESSEE AQUARIUM • CHATTANOOGA

Wish you could've gone a little further south for your vacation? Well, visit the Tennessee Aquarium, the only place in landlocked Tennessee where you can enjoy a tropical vacation—even in the dead of winter. The twelve-story aquarium is the world's largest freshwater aquarium. It holds more than one million gallons of water and is home to 12,000 animals representing 350 species.

In the new Ocean Journey section, you can enjoy more than one hundred feet of lush shoreline, where you can pet sharks

The Tennessee Aquarium is home to 12,000 animals and 350 species.
Photo by Todd Staley/Courtesy of Chattanooga CVB.

and stingrays. Glide through a rainforest butterfly garden and be surrounded by thousands of flutteries. And that's only one of the Aquarium's attractions. From there you'll visit the River Journey. There's the Appalachian cove forest, a Mississippi Delta forest, and a tropical rainforest, filled with the birds and flora of their respective native areas.

One of the Aquarium's most popular tours is the behind-the-scenes tour, where visitors can go backstage and see what it's like to feed 12,000 animals every day and what it's like to clean a 1.1 million gallon fish tank. You'll get to explore the hidden maze of pipes and pumps that keep the water flowing, and find out how to make seawater from scratch. The tours are available Monday through Friday.

Located at 1 Broad Street.

Oh, man! Is nothing sacred? Since 1996, the Nun Bun, a cinnamon bun that bore an uncanny resemblance to Mother Teresa, had graced the counter of the Bongo Java coffee shop. It gained national attention, with features on national news shows, the <u>Late Show with David Letterman</u>, and episodes of <u>The Nanny</u> and <u>Mad About You</u>. Shop owner Bob Bernstein even made a few bucks off it, selling T-shirts and mugs, until Mother Teresa herself wrote a letter asking him to stop.

To preserve the bun (and its attraction to his shop, no doubt) Bernstein had the bun shellacked and displayed prominently under glass. And for nine years it sat there. But then, on Christmas Day 2005, Bernstein opened his shop and with a shock found that the Nun Bun was gone! Stolen! Right from under the glass! The thief took only the bun, leaving the money in the charity bins untouched.

Bernstein reported the theft to the police, but he doesn't hold out much hope for a recovery. Yes, folks, it looks like the Nun Bun is done.

Strange Museums

There's a strong sense of history in Tennessee, as evidenced by the large number of museums throughout the state. But you won't find works by Picasso or Monet gracing these walls. Nah. We're much more interesting than that.

AMERICAN MUSEUM OF SCIENCE AND ENERGY • OAK RIDGE

If we were looking for a truly strange museum (and we were) to kick off our Strange But True tour of museums, we couldn't have found one stranger than this.

Formerly known as the American Museum of Atomic Energy (the name was changed in 1978), the American Museum of Science and Energy opened in 1949 in an old wartime cafeteria with a mission to educate the world on the development of nuclear weaponry, the evolution of nuclear and other types of

The American Museum of Science and Energy educates visitors on the history of nuclear weaponry.
Courtesy of the American Museum of Science and Energy.

energy, and the role of little Oak Ridge, Tennessee, in the development of nuclear weapons.

The museum touts the development of the bombs that effectively ended World War II. Also, the array of new-age solar energy panels on the museum's roof is boasted to be "one of the largest solar power arrays in the Southeast."

Museum programs include a history of Oak Ridge, the secret city, and the vital role it played in World War II-era National Defense.

Located at 300 South Tulane Avenue.

ARCHIE CAMPBELL MUSEUM • BULL'S GAP

No doubt about it, Bull's Gap's favorite son was multi-talented. During his life, he was a country music recording artist, scriptwriter, comedian, sculptor, poet, artist, and reportedly a two-handicap golfer.

Campbell began his career in entertainment as a radio announcer on WNOX in Knoxville in 1936, where he first worked with country music great Roy Acuff. After a break to serve in the Navy during World War II, he began working for a show called *Country Playhouse*, a radio show that became Knoxville's first country music television show. Then, it was on to Nashville and *The Grand Ole Opry*, where he was a comedian on the *Prince Albert* [pipe tobacco] *Show*. That same year— 1958—he launched his career as a comedic recording artist.

In 1969, Campbell joined the cast of *Hee Haw* as a cast member and a writer, where he created a wide cast of zany characters and skits. The show was a big ol' country hit, making

Kornfield Kounty, and its cast household names—at least in the country's rural areas. Campbell became especially popular for his hilarious "spoonerisms"—well-known fairy tales recited with cleverly mispronounced words and mixed up syllables. He was named 1969 Comedian of the Year by the Country Music Association. He remained an active performer and speaker until his death in 1987.

The Archie Campbell Museum is filled with artifacts of Campbell's life, including his childhood home, which was relocated here, and career memorabilia.

Located at 139 South Main Street.

BATTLES FOR CHATTANOOGA ELECTRIC MAP AND MUSEUM • CHATTANOOGA

Talk about strange but true! Experience the sights and sounds of Chattanooga's historical Civil War battles as they unfold before you in lights on the really funky electric map. You enter the small theater and take your seat in front of a diorama of Lookout Mountain, surrounding forests, and the Tennessee River. Dramatic lighting frames the scene and illuminates the five thousand miniature blue and gray clad soldiers covering the diorama.

Entrance music sounds, and a booming voice begins relating a play-by-play account of each battle. Lights blink (there's 650 of 'em), simulating gunfire and marking each battle site. You marvel as the Lilliputian soldiers march and fight and die across the three-dimensional map. And all the while, your senses are being assaulted by the sound of gunfire and other sounds of battle through the museum's "Digital Phase Sound System." Far out!

According to museum history, the electric map was built in 1930-something by unknown hands. Installed in a small building on the side of Lookout Mountain it was billed as the Confederama and opened to the public. Two Confederate flags and "Yankees beware!" warnings were painted on the side of the building. This strong Southern slant made it a popular tourist attraction during the 1960s, the one hundredth anniversary of the Civil War.

By the 1990s, it had fallen to disrepair, but was rescued by Civil War enthusiasts. The map was rewired, repainted, and thoroughly revamped and moved to its present building further down Lookout Mountain. The "Confederama" was dropped, the map became simply "electric," and its new name was unveiled.

Located at 1110 East Brow Road on Lookout Mountain.

BEALE STREET SUBSTATION POLICE MUSEUM • MEMPHIS

Housed in an authentic police precinct, the Beale Street Substation Police Museum makes a unique attraction. It's a must-see for all you "criminalia" fans.

The museum features a history of the Memphis Police Department, which Lord knows, has had its successes and tribulations through the years. In 1932, Memphis gained international notoriety when it was named the Murder Capital of the World. There were 102 homicides committed that year.

The very next year, however, brought a modicum of redemption. An investigation conducted in Memphis in

September 1933 revealed that the infamous gangster and bank robber George "Machine Gun" Kelly and his wife Kathryn were holed up in Memphis. On September 26, FBI agents from Birmingham, Alabama, and Memphis police conducted an early morning raid on the outlaw's hideout. Caught unawares and without his legendary machine gun, Kelly surrendered shouting, "Don't shoot, G-men! Don't shoot!"

The Memphis Police Department's darkest day may well have been April 4, 1968. On that date, Civil Rights Leader Martin Luther King Jr. was delivering a speech in support of a strike by Memphis sanitation workers. As he stood on the balcony of the Lorraine Motel, an assassin's bullet cut him down. Memphis police were put on alert for a "well dressed white man" who was said to have dropped a rifle after the shooting and escaped in a blue car. But James Earl Ray eluded officers and escaped to London, where he was captured four days later.

The Beale Street Substation Police Museum contains exhibits relating to the triumphant capture of Machine Gun Kelly and the tragedy of King's assassination. There are also records of not-so-famous criminals and events that have marked Memphis's history. There are motorcycles, badges, and guns. And you can get your picture taken in the authentic Beale Street pokey. Yikes!

Located at 159 Beale Street.

Strange Museums

BUFORD PUSSER HOME AND MUSEUM • ADAMSVILLE

The rest of the world may have forgotten Sheriff Buford Pusser, but in McNairy County, he's still Walking Tall. Pusser was the straight-talking, big-stick-wielding sheriff who in the 1960s vowed to clean up McNairy County and run all the bad guys out of the state.

He had his work cut out for him. At that time, McNairy was corrupt, rife with crooked politicians (is that redundant?), violent moonshiners determined to continue their illicit business, and, according to Pusser, organized crime.

Pusser, a big man at six feet, six inches and 250 pounds, waded into the dirty pool and stirred up a tsunami. His motto was "Walk tall and carry a big stick." He did both. Swinging that big stick, he began gaining dangerous enemies from every corner of the county.

As his enemies grew, so did his reputation. People marveled when he fought off six men, putting three in jail and three in the hospital. When he destroyed eighty-seven whiskey stills in one year, when he killed two people in self-defense, and when he was shot eight times and stabbed seven, he kept on swinging his way into living legend status.

Pusser paid dearly for his status as a living legend. His wife, who had insisted on accompanying him on an early morning call, was killed by some of his enemies. Pusser himself was shot in the head but survived.

Pusser's exploits reached the ears of a Memphis songwriter and soon he was immortalized in song. It was just a short step from there to the silver screen. The movie, titled *Walking Tall*, made Pusser a household name for a while, and he began making public appearances throughout the country. Plans for a sequel were underway, when tragedy struck. Pusser died in a car wreck on August 21, 1974, at age thirty-six.

The sequels to *Walking Tall* kept Pusser's legend alive for years after his death. A Buford Pusser Festival is held every year in Adamsville, Pusser's hometown. In addition, his home has been opened as a museum, which includes all his furnishings, pictures, memorabilia, and the car he drove as sheriff. Of special interest is a rack hanging on the wall of the Buford Pusser home. It's a rack that would ordinarily hold rifles, but instead it holds a number of Pusser's "big sticks."

The Buford Pusser Home and Museum is located at 342 Pusser (where else?) Street.

CARBO'S POLICE MUSEUM • PIGEON FORGE

You say you didn't see enough weapons and other police paraphernalia at Beale Street and the Buford Pusser Museum? Then, let us tell you about Carbo's Police Museum.

Founded by Dr. and Mrs. Bert Carbo in 1976.

Carbo's Police Museum was founded in 1976.
Courtesy of Carbo's Police Museum.

Strange Museums

Carbo's is dedicated to all law enforcement officers. It has more than five thousand items on display and boasts of having the world's largest authentic exhibit of Sheriff Buford Pusser memorabilia. You'd think that honor would go to the Buford Pusser Museum, but, hey, they only have the car that Pusser used to patrol in. Carbo's has on display, up close and personal, the very 1974 Chevrolet Corvette that Pusser died in! You can even see and hear the big man himself on video—which, of course, you can purchase in the souvenir shop on your way out.

You'll also find a unique private collection of police items, including badges, uniforms, billy clubs, handcuffs, and weapons, lots and lots of weapons.

Located at 3311 Parkway.

The Carter House • Franklin

The Battle of Franklin has been called the Gettysburg of the West for the number of casualties inflicted during it. The Carter House, a modest brick home, was caught smack dab in the middle of the battle.

The Carter House still bears bullet holes from the Battle of Franklin.
Courtesy of the Carter House Museum.

It all began on the evening of November 30, 1864, when the house was commandeered by Union troops. The Carter family, roused from their beds, took refuge in the basement and listened throughout the next day as the battle raged around them.

They heard gunfire, the sound of bullets hitting their home, and the screams of dying men. Hand-to-hand combat was waged on the porch and throughout the rooms of the house. Soldiers were bayoneted on the front steps and clubbed to death in the yard, with canon and gun smoke so thick it was hard to tell just who to shoot. Time after time Confederates charged the Union position, only to be repulsed each time.

After the battle, the Carters climbed from the basement to the carnage of "the bloodiest hours of the American Civil War." More than twenty-five hundred Union soldiers and seven thousand Confederates lost their lives, including the Carter's son Theodric (Tod), who was serving with the Confederacy.

Not suprisingly, the house is now believed to be haunted by some of those who died there. Reportedly, Tod has been seen in that first floor bedroom, sitting on the side of the bed. He's visible for just seconds, and then he disappears. However, Tod is only seen infrequently. The most active ghost seems to be the spirit of Annie Carter, Tod's little sister.

A mischievous sort, she is often felt tugging at a visitor's sleeve or appearing and disappearing in a playful manner. It's been reported that on one occasion, during a guided tour of the house, a statue behind the guide began jumping up and down. Annie is blamed for that little prank.

Restored and opened to the public in 1953, the Carter House has the ignominious distinction of being the most battle-damaged building in the Civil War. Today, a Registered Historic Landmark, it operates as a museum and serves as a memorial to the Carter family and the soldiers who died there. Visit and you can actually stick your finger into holes left by the hundreds of bullets that struck the house during the battle.

Located at 1140 Columbia Avenue.

CASEY JONES VILLAGE AND CASEY JONES HOME/MUSEUM • JACKSON

John Luther "Casey" Jones was a legendary train engineer, who, according to legend, sacrificed his life to save the lives of his passengers. Course that's not everyone's take on the tale. Seems the official accident report settles the blame for the wreck that killed him entirely on Jones's broad shoulders.

By all accounts, Jones was a bear of a man, six foot with a heart as big as his biceps. The consummate engineer, he had distinctive flair

The Casey Jones Museum is one of Tennessee's Top Ten tourist attractions.
Courtesy of the Casey Jones Museum.

with the train whistle, starting it out softly, increasing it to the wail of a banshee, and then drifting off to soft again. Anyone hearing that trademark whistle knew that Casey Jones was coming through. And they knew he'd be coming in on time, for Jones was a stickler about meeting his schedule.

On that fateful night—April 29, 1900—Jones had come into Memphis on his regular run, on time, of course, and was looking forward to an evening at home. But when he learned a fellow engineer was sick and was unable to make his run, Jones agreed to go—on two conditions: That he drive the 382, his regular engine, and that he have Sim Webb, his favorite fireman.

With both conditions met, Jones set out for Canton, Mississippi, almost two hours behind schedule. Ah, but not for long. You see, he had a fast engine, a good fireman, and a light train, all the conditions needed for a record setting run. By highballing (going fast and taking risks) the whole way, he knew he could make up lost time and maybe break a record or two. And, by golly, he would've, too, except for that one itty bitty problem. He squealed his way around a corner just outside of Vaughn, Mississippi, and what to his wondering eyes should appear, but a stalled freight train and six great big train cars. Knowing he'd never be able to stop in time, he screamed for his fireman to jump and save himself, and grabbed the whistle cord in one hand, the brake in the other.

Now here's where the legend gets a bit iffy. You see, once the brake's set, there's not much else an engineer can do, and Jones could've jumped to safety and the outcome would've pretty much been the same. But he stayed, heroically, many say, hoping to do something more to save his passengers. Guess it worked, since Jones was the only one to die that day. Legend has it that when he was removed from the engine, one hand was still clutching the whistle and the other held fast to the brake.

Whatever the truth, it's a good story, and one that's celebrated in Jackson. Casey Jones Village is one of Tennessee's Top Ten tourist attractions. Located at 56 Casey Jones Lane.

CHATTANOOGA CHOO CHOO MODEL RAILROAD MUSEUM • CHATTANOOGA

The Model Railroad Museum contains one of, if not the largest, working model railroad exhibits in the world. The track is 174 feet long and thirty-three feet across at its widest point. The train, which has 120 locomotives of all types, a thousand freight cars, and eighty passenger cars, loops through a miniature world portraying Chattanooga and the Cumberland Mountain Country. There are more than 320 structures, three thousand

The Chattanooga Choo-choo Railroad Museum has one of the largest working model railroad museums in the world.
Courtesy of Chattanooga CVB.

feet of track, 150 switches, three major yards, two small yards, and four passenger stations. It's a kid's paradise!

Located at 1400 Market Street

DRAGON DREAMS DRAGON MUSEUM • CHATTANOOGA

We thought dragons were the stuff of nightmares, but apparently we were wrong. Seems instead they're all about fantasy and fun and the people who love them, at least that's what they say at the one-of-a-kind Dragon Dreams Museum.

The museum is home to a unique collection of dragons. But don't worry—there's no fire-breathing going on. These are friendly dragons. Of course, the fact that they're inanimate may have something to do with it. Anyway, there are eight rooms filled with all manners of dragons.

Dragon Dreams is the brainchild of owner Barbara Newton. She says the museum evolved when her home became too crowded with her private collection of dragons. The dragons were getting lonely. They're meant to be seen and shared, she reasons.

Located at 6724-A East Brainerd Road.

DUKES OF HAZZARD MUSEUM—COOTER'S PLACE • GATLINBURG

Yeeee Haaaw! Y'all grab yore hats and rush on over to Cooter's Place to take a gander at all the *Dukes of Hazzard* stuff he's collected. Why, Ol' Cooter (actor Ben Jones) has so much of Bo and Luke's stuff that he's had to start himself one of those museums. You know where they have really neat stuff, like that woman in Georgia that's got Elvis's wart? Well, Cooter ain't got warts, but he's got the next best thing—the Rocking General Lee—a wood sculpture of Bo and Luke's famous car. The sculpture has rockers, like a rocking chair and a long steering wheel protruding from the hood. It's "a real treasure."

You'll also find Cooter's wrecker, clothing, hats, pictures, news clippings, and lots of other *Dukes of Hazzard* memorabilia. There's even a detached car hood that been airbrushed with a cool *Dukes of Hazzard* scene!

Located at 2613 McGavock Pike.

ELVIS MUSEUM • PIGEON FORGE

There's something in that old adage "You can't keep a good man down." Y'all! This man's been dead since 1977. Geez! Disco was in! And still we won't let him RIP.

Now don't go crying in the chapel. Really, we don't mean to be cruel (hee hee). We'll let you in on a little secret. If you're still all shook up over losing the King, get yourself on over to the Elvis Museum. You won't find the King there, but you will find the next best thing—the King's stuff! And, wow, what stuff! Cars! Jewels! Hair brushes!

Museum founder Mike Moon began collecting Elvis stuff way back in 1971. Seems that upon meeting Elvis he complimented him on his belt and the King, generous heart that he was, whipped off the belt and presented to the Moon. He did that a lot; you know, whipped off things and gave them to friends and strangers alike. It was from that one lone belt that Moon built his collection to what it is today—the World's

Largest Private Collection of Elvis Memorabilia. And he's got it all displayed for you in the three thousand square-foot museum.

There are smoking jackets, tour jackets, sports clothes, guitars, toiletries (with all his money, he used Brut, a $2 cologne), hairbrushes, hair dryers, his Prell shampoo, ACE bandages to wrap his ankles when they swelled, and even his albuterol asthma inhaler. It's an Elvis lover's paradise.

You can even do an overnighter and stay in the TCB luxury suite. It's decorated in "Elvis motif," which, judging by his taste in other stuff, we figure is early kitsch.

So, wipe off that hound dog expression, slap on those blue suedes, and get on over there. You can't help fallin' in love with the place!

Located at 2638 Parkway.

FARRAGUT FOLKLIFE MUSEUM • FARRAGUT

This museum is a treasure trove of artifacts and photographs of the history of the Farragut community. So? Well, as you might guess from the name, Farragut was the hometown of David Farragut, the very first commissioned admiral of the U.S. Navy. We guess he's famous for that, but we know that most folk remember him for his Civil War quote during the Battle of Mobile: "Damn the torpedoes! Full speed ahead!"

One of the highlights of the Farragut Folklife Museum is the nationally recognized Farragut collection, which houses personal artifacts, such as china, uniform ornamentation, manuscripts, letters, family photographs, and a large collection of scrimshaw.

Strange Museums

Additionally, the museum features items from the Farragut and Concord communities, including railroad artifacts, community photographs, and histories of the schools, churches, and changing exhibits of interest.

Located within the Farragut Town Hall at 11408 Municipal Center Drive.

FIRE MUSEUM OF MEMPHIS • MEMPHIS

Here's a hot tip for all you fire buffs out there. OK, we admit we thought fire buffs was another word for arsonists, but apparently not, for the Fire Museum of Memphis is an attraction that "appeals to children, families, fire buffs, conventioneers, and tourists." That just about covers everyone, huh?

Anyway, housed in Fire Engine House No. 1, a restored 1910 fire station, the museum features exhibits that educate visitors about the history of firefighting from the nineteenth century bucket brigades to present day. This exhibit includes a presentation by Ol' Billy, the talking fire horse, who explains what it was like to fight fire in the early days, when the fire trucks were still horse drawn. A collection of fire engines is on display here. Memphis Fire Department Education Specialists are always on duty to discuss fire safety with visitors.

The museum, which is largely funded by fire personnel, features interactive exhibits, complete with fire trucks to ride in and a firefighter's pole to slide down. There are also exhibits on emergency medicine, black firefighters, and historic fires. As you leave, take a moment to peruse the Memorial Wall dedicated to Memphis firefighters who have died in the line of duty.

Located at 118 Adams Avenue.

GUINNESS WORLD OF RECORDS MUSEUM • GATLINBURG

The Fire Museum of Memphis is a restored firehouse from 1910. Courtesy of the Fire Museum of Memphis.

Amazing Exhibits to Captivate at Fun Museum! Hundreds of astounding exhibits! An incredible lineup of feats, facts, and records in an amazing display of unparalleled entertainment!

OK, the exclamation points are ours, but the words are pure Guinness. And there's more! Dramatic recreations come to life! Witness breathtaking wonders of nature! See authentic memorabilia from celebrity record holders like the famous Elvis "Hound Dog" boat! Compare your height to the tallest man! See the most expensive car! See the Batmobile! NEW Interactive Game Shows! New Action Show—Ride the Records! Awesome Achievements! All are designed to amaze! Astound! Delight! And enlighten! Huh? Enlighten? That's what it says…enlighten!

Guess that just about says it all! You can't pass up enlightenment!

Located in the Baskins Square Mall on the Parkway.

THE HERMITAGE • NASHVILLE

The Hermitage is the home of Andrew Jackson, who bought it as a two-story log farmhouse in 1804. Despite the fact that he had grown the farm into a prosperous one thousand acre plantation with new outbuildings, such as a distillery, dairy, carriage shelter, cotton, gin, and slave cabins, Jackson and his wife continued to live in the farmhouse until the winter of 1821.

At that time, a Federal-style two-story brick house was completed, along with formal gardens and more outbuildings. Jackson took office as the seventh U.S. President in 1829 and while in office, he had

The Hermitage was the home of President Andrew Jackson.
Courtesy of the Ladies' Hermitage Association.

the mansion dramatically enlarged, with flanking one-story wings, a two-story entrance portico with Doric columns, and a small rear portico. He also had a Grecian "temple and monument" built for wife Rachel, who had died in 1828.

A chimney fire seriously damaged the mansion in 1834, and it was rebuilt into a stately Greek Revival-style monument.

Jackson returned in 1837 and died there in 1845. He was laid to rest in the tomb next to Rachel.

The Ladies Hermitage Association, a group interested in preserving the Hermitage, acquired the mansion and set about restoring it, the original two-story farmhouse, and an adjacent church. It's through their continuing efforts that the Hermitage was restored and now contains most of its original furnishings. It's operated as a museum, with daily tours throughout the year.

Periodic living history events are conducted as well. Holiday tours, conducted in late November through January 1 by guides in period costumes, feature a look into the Christmas traditions of the Jackson family, showcasing the traditions of the 1800s. A special children's Christmas workshop is also held one Saturday in December. The children learn how children celebrated Christmas at the Hermitage and make crafts to take home.

INTERNATIONAL TOWING AND RECOVERY HALL OF FAME AND MUSEUM • CHATTANOOGA

You can tell from their mission statement that these guys are serious. And we quote:

> Our Mission is to preserve the history of the towing and recovery industry, to educate the children of the world, and of society, about said industry, and to honor those individuals who have made significant changes, and have dedicated precious time throughout our industry.

On their website, they bid you to (and we're quoting again) "Come walk among early towing and recovery history...Enjoy restored antique wreckers and equipment, industry related displays of collectible toys, tools, unique equipment, and pictorial histories of manufacturers who pioneered a worldwide industry..."

Who knew? Who knew there was an International Towing and Recovery Hall Fame? And, who knew they'd be such a serious sort? Really, who in the world would be interested but other tow men, uh tow persons?

International Towing and Recovery Hall of Fame is filled with antique tow trucks.
Courtesy of the ITRHF.

Well...actually...Though their prose may be a bit over-earnest, their museum and Hall of Fame is filled with some pretty neat antique tow trucks, all beautifully restored. There's the newly acquired 1929 Packard tow truck with a Weaver crane and the 1929 Chrysler with a Weaver crane. They are a "dream come true" for the museum.

There's also a collection of early towing equipment antique toy towing trucks dating back to the early 1900s. Oh!

And if you're lucky, museum manager Frank Thomas will give you a personalized tour and regale you with tales from towing's early days.

Located in the heart of Chattanooga's historic district at 3315 Broad Street.

Chattanooga was chosen as the site for the International Towing and Recovery Hall of Fame and Museum because it was just three and a half miles away that the towing industry was born. Back in 1916, Chattanoogan Earnest Holmes Sr. and ten helpers spent all night using only ropes and blocks tied to trees to recover a friend's overturned Model T from a creek. After that experience, Holmes, who had just opened Chattanooga's first independent garage, had the idea to attach poles onto the frame of 1913 Cadillac truck. He then added a pulley and chain, and voila! The world's first tow truck!

An historical marker on Market Street honors Holmes for his contributions to the towing and recovery industry.

LAUDERDALE COURTS APARTMENT WHERE ELVIS LIVED•
MEMPHIS

Hey, here's a trip that strange but true. Now you can rest your pretty head in the room where Elvis dreamed his dreams of greatness. The owners of Lauderdale Courts have restored 185 Winchester #328, the apartment that the Presleys moved into in 1949, shortly after coming to Memphis from Tupelo. It's "the only place on earth you can stay where Elvis lived."

The 689 square-foot apartment was originally part of the Roosevelt-era WPA housing development. Once slated for demolition, it was rescued, restored, and is now registered on the National Register of Historic Places. And it's up for rent. That is, you can rent it for a nightly fee.

Guests can step back in time, for the restored apartment features vintage furniture and kitchen and bathroom fixtures.

And more! The place is full of Presley family photos and memorabilia.

LITTLE RIVER RAILROAD AND LUMBER COMPANY MUSEUM • TOWNSEND

In the early 1900s, the Little River Railroad operated in the Smoky Mountains, transporting tourists in and taking out the thousands of trees cut by the area's logging companies. The Little River Railroad and Lumber Company Museum was organized to keep alive the stories of these two companies.

You'd think a museum about lumber would be, well, a bit wooden. Not so! True, there are hundreds of photos hanging on the wall that tell the story of the Little River Lumber Company, and hey, there's even a huge saw or two hanging there too. But the photo exhibit is only a small part of this museum.

There are also choo choo trains to see. The outdoor exhibits include a vintage caboose, two vintage flat cars, and a portable steam engine. The exhibits also include a restored "set-off" house, a house used by logging families in the mountains, a refurbished water tower, and a replica passenger platform. Museum volunteers are well versed in knowledge of the railroad and logging operations. They are present for the interpretive exhibits and to share their knowledge of life as a mountain logger or on the railroad.

The Little River Railroad and Lumber Company Museum offers historical tours.
Courtesy of the LRRLCM.

LORETTA LYNN RANCH AND COAL MINER'S DAUGHTER MUSEUM • HURRICANE MILLS

Coal Miner's Daughter. Country Music Icon. Living Legend. These are titles you would, no doubt, associate with singer Loretta Lynn. What about Social Activist? Women's Advocate? No? Well, just listen to a little of her early music.

True, she ain't Betty Friedan. In fact, she once received notoriety for falling asleep during a Betty Friedan interview on the *Dick Frost Show*. But, listen to her music, and you'll hear a working class woman's woman, someone who has lived your life and has put it to music.

She sang about heartache, but it was heartache with triumph—strong women living their lives and dealing with adversity. Her songs dealt with marriage, children, and divorce.

Drinking and cheating husbands were put on notice. Her song "One's On the Way," spoke to the woman overwhelmed by kids, housework, and negligent husbands.

As much notice as those songs brought her, they couldn't compare to her song "The Pill," which talked about a woman discovering the advantages of easy birth control. The song caused much controversy and was banned from many radio stations, but that didn't keep women from listening to it and heeding its message.

The Coal Miner's Daughter Museum is located within the Loretta Lynn Ranch, which is advertised as the seventh largest attraction in Tennessee. Make a day of it. You can tour Lynn's fourteen-room plantation home, nestled amid her thirty-five hundred-acre ranch, with a campground and Western town. Included is a tour of the re-created Butcher Holler home place that the Coal Miner's Daughter grew up in.

The Coal Miner's Daughter Museum contains Lynn's history, from her Butcher Holler, Kentucky, rags to her Nashville, Tennessee, riches. The tale is told in pictures, costumes, posters, awards, manuscripts, handwritten lyrics to hit songs, and other memorabilia. Lots and lots of other memorabilia. The eighteen thousand square-foot museum is packed to the gills with the detritus of Lynn's life, including costumes and personal belongings from her friends, which just happen to be yesterday's country music legends and today's superstars.

If you're lucky, too, you might just visit on a day that the proprietor herself is there, since it's a favorite project of hers.

If so, be sure to ask about the others who live there—the ones you can't see. So many spirits have been identified there, that the house was featured in a Travel Channel special titled *Loretta Lynn's Haunted Plantation*.

Loretta's daughter Peggy remembers her first encounter with one of the house spirits. She was three and was lying in bed, when she felt as if someone was watching her. When she turned, she saw a Lady in White emerging from the bathroom. Peggy remembers wondering who the visitor was when the Lady in White simply vanished.

Loretta herself saw this Lady in White one day. She was on the second floor balcony, wringing her hands and crying. Before Loretta could ask who she was and why she was crying, the Lady in White disappeared. Research uncovered the fact that the house's original mistress, Beulah Anderson, gave birth to a stillborn infant. Beulah died days later and the two were buried in the cemetery on the property. Loretta believes the Lady in White is Beulah, still grieving her dead child.

MUSEUM OF APPALACHIA • NORRIS

The Museum of Appalachia opened in 1962, but it was actually begun many years before that. When founder John Rice Irwin was a boy, his grandfather would show him a collection of "old timey things," family items that dated back many generations. These were things he had hung on to through the years, somehow knowing the importance of preserving them. He told his young grandson he should "start a little museum with these old timey things."

Strange Museums

John Rice inherited not only those old timey things, but also his grandfather's love of history and his conviction that it should be preserved. He did, indeed, start a little museum with this grandfather's old timey things. And he spent many years traveling through the backwoods of Appalachia, meeting people, talking, and gathering many more old timey things to include in his museum.

The Museum of Appalachia is no longer a "little museum." It covers sixty-five acres, with twenty-five buildings and more than a quarter of a million "old timey" items. But you won't find those items displayed in a dusty old museum. Irwin has, instead, re-created a living, breathing Appalachian village, where visitors can take a stroll into Southern Appalachia.

The Museum of Appalachia is full of "old timey things."
Courtesy of the Museum of Appalachia.

Little appears to have changed here since the settlers cleared the land and built their homes. Animals roam the grounds—sheep, goats, cattle, geese, and chickens. The gardens are well tended and the houses are neat. It's as if the family will return any second.

In addition to some thirty log cabins, there's a blacksmith shop, a school, and a church, barns, and smoke houses, all of which are furnished with Southern Appalachian artifacts. The Hall of Fame, Display Barn, and People's Building contain thousands of regional items, including folk art, musical instruments, baskets, toys, and rifles. There's also a Craft, Gift, and Antique shop and a small restaurant that serves home cooking every day.

NATIONAL ORNAMENTAL METAL MUSEUM • MEMPHIS

The National Ornamental Metal Museum in Memphis is truly one of a kind.

The purpose of the museum is to preserve and showcase the artistry of metalworkers from around the world. But don't go expecting to see a collection of fencework. The permanent exhibits feature more than three

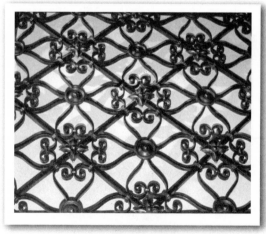

The National Ornamental Metal Museum showcases the creative side of metalworking.
Courtesy of the NOMM.

thousand pieces of fine metal work, some dating back five hundred years or more. You'll see bejeweled knives, intricate gold jewelry, decorative teapots, even barbecue cookers.

Of course, there is fencework, too. The East and West gates of the museum are a favorite of visitors. The gates, sixteen feet high and fifteen feet wide, are two sections of forged steel and scrollwork finished in 23k gold leaf. The decorative rosettes that connect the scrollwork are the work of nearly two hundred different artists. These rosettes, personal statements of the individual artists, take many forms, including fish, musical instruments, teeth, and cowboy hats, just to name a few.

There's also a working blacksmith shop a gift shop! Located at 374 Metal Museum Drive.

Oliver Springs Railroad Depot Museum • Oliver Springs

This restored 1897 railroad depot contains artifacts and photographs of the area's rich mining history. You'll find a restored Southern Railroad caboose, hotel ticket booth, and a horse-drawn fire wagon. The town's library is also located here.

Located in downtown Oliver Springs.

Pink Palace Family of Museums • Memphis

If you grew up in the South you know what folks mean when they say they're "Gonna run on over to the Pig to pick up a few things." The Piggly Wiggly chain of stores was the country's first ever self-service stores. They also were the first to have refrigerated produce cases and national-brand advertising. All these innovations were the creations of Memphis native Clarence Saunders, who opened his first Piggly Wiggly store in 1916 at 79 Jefferson in downtown Memphis. By 1929, they were the second largest group of stores in the nation. Saunders, however, due to a dispute with the New York Stock Exchange, had to declare bankruptcy, though he went on to open two other chain stores. Today, Piggly Wiggly stores can be found throughout the country,

The Pink Palace Museum celebrates Memphis's history from prehistoric times to today.
Courtesy of Memphis CVB.

particularly in the Southeast.

Memphis has another of Saunder's legacies—the Pink Palace, Saunder's dream home, which because of his bankruptcy in 1920, ended up in city hands. The city of Memphis has taken the Pink Palace, so named for its pink Georgian marble façade, and turned it into a whole complex of activity centers.

The Pink Palace Museum is one of the largest facilities of its kind in the Southeast. It's filled with hands-on displays, exciting exhibits, dioramas, and audio-visual presentations. You can learn of Memphis's history. Walk through a replica of the first Piggly Wiggly. What fun! See how dinosaurs and fossils dramatically chronicle our ever-changing planet (their words, not ours). The many interactive exhibits are great for kids and grownups alike. There's an IMAX Theater here—the first in the Southeast—with changing features. The Sharpe Planetarium is also here. Something for everyone! It's a place to spend the day.

Located 3050 Central Avenue.

RAMSEY HOUSE PLANTATION • KNOXVILLE

The Ramsey House was built in 1797 by Thomas Hope, Knoxville's first builder, for Colonel Francis Ramsey, whose family was one of the first to settle in Knoxville. Colonel Ramsey was a founding trustee of Blount College, now the University of Tennessee.

The Ramsey House Plantation has been restored, with original interior and exterior

The Ramsey House Plantation was built in 1797. Courtesy of KTSC/Ramsey House Plantation.

architectural features. It has the first attached kitchen in Tennessee, added five years after the home was built. The attached kitchen replaced the typical "dog-trot" Southern style, where the kitchen was a stand-alone with a breezeway from the house.

The home is entirely furnished with period furniture and house wares, with many items owned by the Ramsey family, including a pair of Chippendale chairs that were a gift to Colonel Ramsey and a set of handmade dolls once belonging to Eliza Ramsey.

The plantation's one hundred acres, which includes the Heritage Gardens, is open to the public. You can bring a picnic and feel free to roam.

The plantation is listed on the National Registry of Historic Places. Located at 2614 Thorngrove Pike.

SALT AND PEPPER SHAKER MUSEUM • GATLINBURG

Holy salt cellar, Batman! It's a whole museum of salt and pepper shakers! When Andrea Ludden began her search for a working pepper mill some twenty years ago,

The Salt and Pepper Shaker Museum is home to seventeen thousand salt and pepper shakers. Courtesy of Andrea Ludden.

she never planned to someday be opening the world's only salt and pepper shaker museum. But, here she is with more than seventeen thousand of the little suckers.

The museum is a bit of kitschy fun, and, hey, on your way

out, you can add to your own salt and pepper shaker collection in the gift shop, well stocked with vintage and new items.

Located in the Winery Square at 461 Brookside Village Way.

SEQUOYAH BIRTHPLACE MUSEUM • VONORE

Sequoyah was a Cherokee who enlisted on the side of the United States to fight the British and the Creek Indians in the War of 1812. It was then that he became aware of the importance of the written word, for unlike the white soldiers, the Cherokee lacked a written language. They were unable to write home, to read military orders or record events.

When Sequoyah returned home, he began work on a writing system for the Cherokee. He finally reduced the thousands of Cherokee thoughts to eighty-five symbols representing sounds, and after twelve years of work he introduced the system to the Cherokee people. Within months, thousands of Cherokee became literate.

As the inventor of the Cherokee written language, Sequoyah is the only person in recorded history to develop an entire alphabet. The Cherokee Nation honored him by striking a silver medal in his honor and presenting him with a lifelong pension. He served his people as a diplomat and statesman throughout his life.

The Sequoyah Museum, Tennessee's only tribally owned historic attraction, presents the story of Sequoyah. There are also displays of Cherokee history and culture and gardens that demonstrate Cherokee agriculture and gardening practices from the fourteenth century.

Located at 576 Highway 360.

University of Memphis Institute of Egyptian Art and Archaeology • Memphis

We've got this all wrapped up. Yeah, yeah. It's a weak mummy joke. The Institute's collection contains more than one hundred and fifty objects, including mummies, religious and funerary (love that word!) items, jewelry, and everyday objects.

One of the most mundane, yet interesting, of those everyday items is a four thousand-year-old loaf of bread that was placed under the foundation of Mentuhotep II's mortuary temple in ancient Thebes. Meant to symbolize the importance of abundant food in the afterlife, the loaf contains sand and small stones, which became part of the bread during the bread making process. These gritty elements wore down the tooth enamel of ancient Egyptians and led to abscesses, the main reason for their tooth loss. Interesting, huh?

The art museum is located in the Communication and Fine Arts Building, Room 142 at 3750 Norriswood Avenue. The Institute of Egyptian Art and Archeology is located at 201 Jones Hall.

The Haunting of Tennessee

Mist rising on moonlit nights. Ghostly apparitions floating through hallowed halls. Strange and scary noises. Tennessee can be a spooky place at night. With a past so rich in history, it's no wonder there are haints wandering this land. Here's just a smattering of Tennessee's legendary ghost tales.

THE BELL WITCH • ADAMS

The Bell Witch is, without a doubt, one of America's most famous ghosts. Her story began in 1817 on the John Bell farm in tiny Adams. According to legend, strange things began happening in the home of the prosperous Bell family. It started with rapping, knocking, and scratching noises.

Blankets were pulled from the bed and family members were kicked, scratched, and had their hair pulled. Betsy, John's twelve-year-old daughter, seemed particularly singled out. She was scratched, stuck with pins, and bruised.

After John Bell let folks in on what was happening, the spirit revealed herself as the witch, Kate Batts, a neighbor of the Bell's, with whom John had had a bad business deal over a group of slaves he'd bought.

Kate began making daily appearances at the Bell's home, generally wreaking havoc on all members. She said her plan was to kill John and to keep Betsy from marrying the fellow she was in love with. According to the legend, John did indeed fall ill of a mysterious illness, for which Kate took credit. While he was abed and ill, Kate constantly harassed him, keeping him from resting. At his funeral, Kate continued her harassment, laughing, cursing, and singing as he was buried.

After his death, Kate turned her attentions to Betsy, threatening her until she dropped her plans to marry her true love. The ghost, so active and so vocal, soon became notorious.

She became so well known that reportedly, General Andrew Jackson visited the Bell Farm to meet Kate. While there, he heard Kate and experienced her mischievousness, when the wheel of his carriage would not turn until Kate let them. Said Jackson: "By the eternal, I saw nothing, but I heard enough to convince me that I would rather fight the British than to deal with this torment they call the Bell Witch!"

The Bell Witch finally left the family, but with a promise to return in seven years. She reportedly did return, appearing to John Bell Jr. long enough to predict the Civil War and both World Wars. She promised to return in 107 years—1935. That year came and went, however, without an appearance.

Local residents aren't so sure she's gone, though. They think she now inhabits the small cave, called the Bell Witch Cave, located on the former Bell Farm. Weird happenings have been reported there, and the current owners, who also report strange apparitions and unexplained sounds, open the cave for tourists. Appointments are necessary.

Numerous stories and books have been written about the Bell Witch, and many a website has been created in her honor.

There's even a movie, *Bell Witch: The Movie*, which incorporates the Bell Witch legend into an entirely new story—your classic scream flick. The movie premiered September 24, 2005 to a sold out crowd at Nashville's Ryman Auditorium. We're bettin' ol' Kate was there too.

CARNTON MANSION • FRANKLIN

Remember way back in the previous section when we told you about the Battle of Franklin and how the Carter House was smack dab in the middle of the battle? Well, ditto that on the Carnton Mansion. OK, so this house, owned by John McGavok, may have only been dab in the middle, but, hey, that's pretty darn close.

Seems that late in the afternoon of November 30, 1864, mistress of the house, Carrie McGavok, began hearing guns and canon fire and the screams of dying

The Carnton Mansion served as a military hospital during the Civil War.
Courtesy of the Historic Carnton Plantation.

men, and she knew a battle was going on nearby. Night fell, but the battle continued apace until midnight when rain and sleet began to fall.

The Haunting of Tennessee

As wounded men gathered near Carnton, Carrie ordered the servants to roll up the carpets (all that blood wouldn't be good for them, ya know) and to help the wounded inside. More than two hundred wounded soldiers were brought inside, where Carrie and her servants tore up clothing for bandages and fed as many as she could. Doctors came and set up a hospital, using the parlor as an operating room.

The dead were carried out to the back of the house. Reportedly, there were so many dead soldiers that they had to be stood erect side by side. Carrie recorded information about the dead, preserving names, initials, or just items that the men carried in hopes of comforting their grieving families. Days later, the Confederate Army buried hundreds of soldiers outside the nearby Carter House.

However, in 1866, John McGavok saw that the graves were deteriorating. He set aside two acres of Carnton Plantation for the largest privately owned Confederate cemetery. There were 1,496 bodies re-interred here, in order by state. Carrie's meticulous burial records were used to place markers over the soldiers that were known. John and Carrie maintained the cemetery for the rest of their lives.

With so much death here, it's no wonder that Carnton Mansion has been called "the most haunted building in Tennessee." Ghost stories abound. The most well-known ghost is that of the restless soldier who wanders through the house and across the back porch. He's also been seen walking through the yard. The sound of his heavy boots accompanies each sighting.

There are reports of other spirits too, including the McGavok's cook, a young girl who was killed in the 1840s, and a ghost who likes to break glass. There are also reports of a woman in white—perhaps Carrie herself—who is often seen wandering through the mansion.

Carnton Mansion has been restored and is open to the public for guided tours. It has received much national notice recently. The story of Carnton was recounted in the PBS docudrama *Southern Haunts*. Additionally, *The Widow of the South*, a novel based on Carrie McGavok and her heroics during the Civil War, recently spent five weeks on the New York Times Bestseller List.

Carnton Mansion is located at 1345 Carnton Lane.

CHICKAMAUGA-CHATTANOOGA MILITARY PARK • CHATTANOOGA

This military park, the site of the Battles for Chattanooga, is said to be haunted by…something. Nicknamed "Old Green Eyes," the thing is said to be a cape-wearing humanoid creature with green-orange glowing eyes, fanglike teeth, and waist-length hair. It's been spotted by rangers and

Chickamauga-Chattanooga Military Park is believed to be the home of goblins and ghouls. Courtesy of the CCMP.

park visitors. In the 1970s, the creature was blamed for causing two car accidents, when the drivers said they spotted it on the side of the road. We just wonder what bar they'd been in before...

The park is also said to be haunted by a lady in white (ever notice how it's always a "Lady in White?"), who is often seen roaming the grounds. It's speculated that she's searching for her dead sweetheart who died in one of the battles here.

CRAIGMILES BLOODY MAUSOLEUM • CLEVELAND

During the Civil War, John Craigmiles, an astute businessman and prosperous Cleveland resident, was tapped to serve as the chief of the commissary agent for the Confederacy, an apt post, since he had made his fortune in the supply business. He served in this capacity for the entire war, and during this time, he managed to hang onto most of his fortune by shunning paper money and trading only in gold.

After the war, tragedy seemed to follow the Craigmiles family. It began in 1871, with the death of Nina, seven-year-old daughter of John and wife, Adelia. Nina was killed when a train struck the carriage in which she was riding.

Grief stricken, John built an elaborate mausoleum for his beloved Nina's body. It's a grand white marble structure, located behind St. Luke's Episcopal Church, with walls four-feet thick. A spire topped with a cross rises thirty-seven feet from the ground. Six shelves were built into the mausoleum with a marble sarcophagus set in the center for Nina.

Not long after Nina was interred, dark red stains appeared on the white marble of the mausoleum. They were scrubbed, but would not go away.

Tragedy struck the Craigmiles again when his infant son died within hours of his birth. John was next, succumbing to a freak case of blood poisoning in 1899. And finally, Adelia was killed when she was struck by a car in 1928.

Reportedly, as each family member was placed into the mausoleum, the stains became larger and deeper. Through the years, the stains have been scrubbed, and at one point some of the marble was replaced, but to no avail. The stains reappeared. They're there still. Make a trip to see for yourself.

St. Luke's Episcopal Church is located at 320 Broad Avenue Northwest.

EAST TENNESSEE STATE UNIVERSITY • JOHNSON CITY

The most famous ghost of ETSU is founding president Sidney Gilbreath, who is reported to haunt Gilbreath Hall. Seems he's still taking care of things, closing doors and windows and turning off unnecessary lights. At least one student has claimed to see the former president peering out an upper floor window.

Burleson Hall is also haunted by one of its namesakes. Reportedly, Christine Burleson, a favorite professor of literature for many decades, committed suicide because of a debilitating disease. Her ghost has been blamed for a variety of hauntings, including moaning, disembodied voices, and other strange sounds.

Mathes Hall is reportedly haunted by a ghost that likes to follow the maintenance workers around. Workers report the feeling of being followed and hearing heavy footsteps that stop when they stop. One woman reported hearing mysterious crashing sounds on an upper floor, when she was supposedly alone in the building.

MERIWETHER LEWIS PARK • GORDONSBURG

The spirit of Meriwether Lewis, of Lewis and Clark fame, is believed to haunt this park that is named in his honor. He died here, some say mysteriously, on October 11, 1809. Traveling the Natchez Trace, bound for Washington with his memoirs, which were to be published, he sought shelter for the night at Grinder's Stand, an informal inn owned by the Grinder family.

Mrs. Grinder later reported that Lewis was acting strangely, talking to himself and pacing about, and, indeed, it was known that he suffered an inherited "hypochondrical condition."

Sometime during the night Mrs. Grinder, who was staying at a nearby cabin, reported hearing three shots and soon Lewis was banging on her door, saying he was shot and begging for assistance. She refused to open the door

This is the site where Meriwether Lewis died under mysterious circumstances in 1809.
Courtesy of the National Park Service.

and watched through the peephole as Lewis staggered around, begging for water. From all accounts, he lived several hours, often banging on the cabin door for help.

Mrs. Grinder's refusal to help raised many questions about Lewis's death. She reported that he had committed suicide, shooting himself once in the chest and once in the head (obviously, he was not an ace marksman!), and this was the official ruling. However, the circumstances surrounding the death raised questions, and many believed he was murdered.

The controversy rages still, almost two hundred years later, with various scenarios hotly debated among historians. So, we guess it's no wonder that Meriwether still wanders.

Orpheum Theatre • Memphis

The spirit of a little girl known only as Mary reportedly haunts this grand theatre. Legend has it that after being struck and killed by a car on Beale Street, little Mary moved into the nearby theatre. She's been reported here for more than sixty years.

Patrons throughout the years have reported doors opening and closing, the sounds of phantom giggles, and the tip tap of little feet. Mary has also reportedly been seen sitting in seat number C-5, which seems to be her favorite.

By all accounts, she's never caused a disturbance. In 1977, however, there were so many strange events that the traveling cast of *Fiddler on the Roof* was convinced the place was haunted. They demanded a séance on the upper balcony to try to contact the ghost. Mary's little playful pranks have become commonplace and are expected by theatre employees.

The Haunting of Tennessee

It seems, however, that Mary's got a little company out there in the netherworld. In 1979, a University of Memphis parapsychology class conducted an investigation in the theatre. The class reported evidence of at least six other ghosts.

The Orpheum Theatre in Memphis offers grand architecture and the giggling ghost of a little girl named Mary.
Courtesy of the Orpheum Theatre.

RYMAN AUDITORIUM • NASHVILLE

The Ryman Auditorium doesn't have a Lady in White. Instead, the home of the *Grand Ole Opry*'s got a Man in Gray. No one knows just who this fellow is, but he's been spotted late at night in the Auditorium's balcony section. He disappears before anyone can get to the balcony to find out who he is.

He's not alone. According to legend, the place is also haunted by country music great Hank Williams. Seems that during the last renovation of the building, a worker was accidentally locked in. During the night, while wandering the building, he came face to face with country music great Hank Williams, who died in a car crash in 1953.

In the 1990s, when the *Grand Ole Opry* was moved to Opryland for a short time, the idea to tear down the Ryman was kicked around by Opry officials. Though they deny it, many people believe the Opry officials were eager to tear down the building because of the so-called "Opry Curse."

Those associated with the *Grand Ole Opry* insist that the curse stems from media sensationalism in the 1970s, but others point to

The Ryman Auditorium was once the home of the *Grand Ole Opry*.
Courtesy of the Ryman Auditorium.

the untimely deaths of more than thirty-five people closely associated with the *Opry* up until 1973. These deaths include the murders of *Hee-Haw* comic Stringbean Akeman and performer Jimmy Widener in 1973, and the plane crash deaths of singers Jim Reeves, Patsy Cline, Cowboy Copas, and Randy Hayes. Other deaths involved car crashes, drugs and alcohol, and one smoke inhalation.

The Haunting of Tennessee

WICKHAM STATUES • PALMYRA

From 1952 until his death in 1970, E.T. Wickham labored over a collection of some pretty unusual yard art. Displayed near his home, the large statutes, including Paul Bunyan and his blue ox Babe, JFK, and Patrick Henry, drew in folks interested in viewing Wickham's art. Wickham enjoyed meeting and talking with these people and was quite attached to the statutes.

Many people believe Wickham was so attached to his statues that he's stayed around to protect them. The people who've claimed to have felt his presence say he's a benevolent sort, perhaps too benevolent. In the last few years, vandals have caused significant damage to the statues, which are still standing where Wickham left them thirty years ago.

Reportedly, there are other ghosts wandering the area around Wickham's statues and cabin—a family who lived in the area many years ago. The wife contracted pneumonia and was dying. Her husband, not wanting to see her suffer (uh huh), killed her. When he learned his son had witnessed the…euthanasia?…he killed him as well. Then, in remorse, he killed himself. Supposedly, they are all buried here and continue to roam the area.

Eat, Drink, and Be Merry!

Eating out in Strange But True Tennessee is more than a meal; it's an experience. There are restaurants and bars galore along the back road trails, some historic, some haunted, some just plain fun.

B.B. KING'S BLUES CLUB • MEMPHIS

If you're really, really, really lucky when you visit B.B. King's Blues Club, you might just get in to hear the smoky, lamenting voice of the big man himself. Two times a year, B.B. King, accompanied by the plaintive wails of guitar Lucille, delivers six SRO shows. Unvaryingly, the two give a rousing show, raucously playing

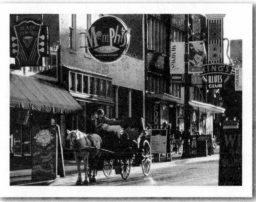

Even if you can't make it for one of King's six shows a year, B.B. King Blues Club always serves a little jazz with their famous gumbo. Courtesy of Memphis CVB.

off each other in performances that repeatedly bring the crowd to its feet, here on Beale Street, where King got his start.

Eat, Drink, and Be Merry!

Even if you're not lucky enough to visit when King and Lucille appear, you'll not be disappointed. Swing and sway on the large dance floor to first-rate blues artists, who perform here every night. And when you work up an appetite on that steamy dance floor, take a break for a little Southern cooking. Award-winning gumbo, fall-off-the-bone ribs, and catfish fried light are just a few of the items found on the menu.

Located at 143 Beale Street.

In the fifty years he's been singing the blues, B.B. King has gone through fifteen guitars, each one of them named Lucille. Ya knew there was a story behind the name, didn'cha?

Seems that in the mid-1950s, King was playing at a dance in Twist, Arkansas. A coupla guys got to scuffling and knocked over a kerosene stove, starting a fire. King ran to safety with the crowd. When he realized he'd left his beloved guitar behind, he ran back inside the blazing building to retrieve it, almost dying in the process.

Later learning the two guys were fighting over a woman named Lucille, he named the guitar in honor of that woman to remind him not to do anything so stupid again. Since then, all King's guitars have been named Lucille.

"She prefers younger men," King says of his current custom Gibson Lucille. "But she puts up with me."

BAKER PETERS JAZZ CLUB • KNOXVILLE

Baker Peters serves up that Nouveau American cuuusseene and good jazz music in equal portions, with just a dash of a ghost story for good measure.

The restaurant lives up to its self-proclamation as "Knoxville's true cosmopolitan restaurant with southern hospitality," with an emphasis on that "cosmopolitan" thing.

The food is so delectable here that reservations are a good idea. Then, again, it's not such a bad thing to wait for a table. You can sip a martini from the extensive martini bar, smoke a cigar from the cigar menu, and groove on a little jazz while you wait in the bar of the beautifully restored Baker-Peters Mansion.

If you turn to find a guy wearing a Confederate uniform sitting next to you, don't panic. Just hand him a cigar and order him a martini. That's Abner Baker, the resident ghost. See, Abner's father, James, built the house back in 1840. Dr. Baker was treating wounded Confederate soldiers at the house, when Union soldiers, alerted to his actions, shot and killed him through a barricaded bedroom door. The bullet holes are still there.

When Abner returned from the war, he killed William Hall, the Knoxville postmaster who allegedly informed on Abner's pa. Shortly thereafter, Abner died—at age twenty-two—in a revenge shooting. He reportedly haunts the house now.

Cool, huh? Fancy food. Good jazz. And a ghost story. What more can ya ask for?

Located at 9000 Kingston Pike.

Eat, Drink, and Be Merry!

BLUEBIRD CAFÉ • NASHVILLE

It's small—just twenty-one tables for reservations. Maybe there'll be room at the bar or on the benches, available on a first-come-first-served basis. But if you got no reservation, you better be first, for the Bluebird Café holds only 110 people and it's one of Nashville's—and music's—premier spots. Small, but with a big, worldwide reputation for the best original country and acoustic music. Playing here, seven nights a week.

But don't come expecting a wild country night. The Bluebird is a listening place. It's not a talking place. If you're looking for conversation, go elsewhere. It's not a jammin' place either. No popular artists playing popular songs. Naw. What you got are undiscovered songwriters, who, since 1985, have been auditioning for the right to play their music for you. And undiscovered artists entertain you with their undiscovered voices on Open Mic night. Undiscovered, huh? So why all the fuss?

Well…let's see. The Bluebird Café is where Garth Brooks used to hang out in the days before his discovery. It's where he performed on Open Mic night before superstardom. It's where he first heard his giant hit "The Dance," written by Tony Arata. It was one of the first songs he recorded after landing a recording contract. He also discovered Larry Bastian's "Unanswered Prayers" and "Rodeo" here.

Kathy Mattea made a name here. Mary Chapin Carpenter debuted on November 10, 1987. The Sweethearts of the Rodeo signed their recording contract here—and got a mention for the Bluebird in the *New York Times*. T. Graham Brown. Vince Gill.

Even the employees get in on the act. Dishwasher/Bartender Mark Irwin wrote Alan Jackson's hit "Here in the Real World," and waitress Liz Henbar wrote Reba McEntire's number one hit "For My Broken Heart."

And country's not all you'll hear. Janis Ian is a regular. So is jazz saxophonist Jay Patten. Hey, even Donna Summer's played here. Back in 1993, she spoofed one of her hit songs, singing "She Works Hard for the Chili."

So make your reservations. Come early. Have a sandwich, maybe some dessert. Then settle back with a beer and listen. You never know what you'll hear.

Located at 4104 Hillsboro Road.

BLUES CITY CAFÉ • MEMPHIS

Like the Bluebird, Blues City Café is not your typical greasy spoon. Oh, they got food, all right. "Come in and put some South in your Mouth," is their slogan. And it's a good slogan, cause they're known for their

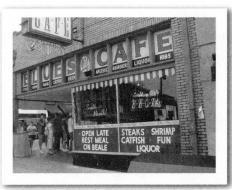

"Come and put a little South in your Mouth" at the Blues City Café, a favorite of celebrities.
Courtesy of the Blues City Café.

outstanding barbecue ribs, homemade hot tamales, Southern-fried catfish, and broiled steaks by the pound. But that's where "typical greasy spoon" ends.

Eat, Drink, and Be Merry!

See, at night, the place gets hopping, with an eclectic blend of live music. Through the years, the Blues City Café's music venue, the Band Box, has hosted a wild array of bands: B.B. King, Jerry Lee Lewis, Hank Williams Jr., Ike Turner, Reverend Al Green, Keanu Reeves and Dogstar, Courtney Love, Queen Latifah, Smashing Pumpkins, Los Lonely Boys. Whew!

That's not all, either. The Blues City Café has an international reputation. It's one of the must-be-seen places when celebrities come to town. On any given night, you might find yourself rubbing elbows with the likes of President Bill Clinton, Bill Murray, or Robert Duvall.

The Blues City Café has been featured on the Food Network's *Bobby Flay Show* and *A Taste of America* on the Travel Channel as well *Bon Apetite* magazine and other food publications. Come on in and put a little South in Your Mouth.

Located at 138 Beale Street.

Beale Street has made many contributions to American culture. One of those is the zoot suit, popular in the 1930s and 1940s swing era. The suit was designed by Beale Street tailor Louis Lettes. The suit's long jacket was designed to keep the suit pants from wearing out or "shining" too soon. The zoot suit became a symbol of the swing era.

BOSCO'S • MEMPHIS

Bosco's is beer. They do food, too. They're famous for their gourmet pizzas, featuring homemade crusts made with whole-wheat flour, olive oil, and a measure of their hand crafted beer, and fresh imported and domestic toppings. Their signature item is fresh salmon baked on a cedar plank in the brick oven. There's double cut pork chops and prime cuts of steak, soups, salads, sandwiches, and desserts, too.

But Bosco's is beer. They have a long history in beer. Besides being the first post-prohibition restaurant brewery in Tennessee, they're internationally recognized as a pioneer in craft brewing. Their innovations include the development of a traditional Stone, or Steinbeer. In this process, pieces of pink Colorado granite are heated to a red-hot 700 degrees in a wood oven and lowered into the unfermented beer during the brewing process. This produces a steam and sizzle that caramelizes the unfermented beer, resulting in a sweeter, softer tasting beer with caramel undertones. The process is varied slightly from location to location. In Memphis, you'll find the Famous Flaming Stone Beer to be sweeter, more caramelized, while Nashville's has a slightly smoky taste.

So, Bosco's is beer. Come and enjoy a good meal. But, please. Don't ask for a Miller Lite.

Located at 2120 Madison Avenue.

BROOKS SHAW'S OLD COUNTRY STORE • JACKSON

When Brooks Shaw suffered a heart attack at age thirty-two and was advised to get a hobby, no one expected his hobby would turn into a collection of more than fifteen thousand antiques from southern general stores. And that his collection would spark the creation of a whole village. But that's what happened.

As a youngster, Shaw worked in a general store for 50 cents a day and all the hoop cheese he could eat. He remembered those days fondly and so, began collecting artifacts from old-timey general stores. By 1965, Shaw's antique collection overflowed his home. So he and wife Annie started an antique museum. Calling it The Old Country Store, they offered cold cuts, cheese and cracker plates, pickles, and the like. Later, an old student union building from nearby Lambuth College was added on to make a restaurant. Shaw's hobby didn't help him a whole lot, considering he died in 1971 at age thirty-eight, but his legacy lives on.

In 1978, the Shaw family moved The Old Country Store to a new location and founded Casey Jones Village, named for local railroad hero Casey Jones.

The Old Country Store is a lot like Brooks Shaw left it. Stepping inside is like stepping back to the 1890s. Thousands of antiques decorate the walls, hang from the ceiling, and cover the floors of the building. These are pieces from Brooks's original collection, gathered from the barns of West Tennessee and back roads antique shops all over the South. It's one of the South's largest private antique collections.

Located at 56 Casey Jones Lane.

CHARLIE VERGO'S RENDEZVOUS • MEMPHIS

This restaurant has been a Memphis tradition since 1948, when Charlie Vergo cleaned out a basement below his diner and made a discovery. There it was—an old coal chute. But this wasn't just any coal chute. This coal chute would give rise to some smokin' good ribs. As a vent for Charlie Vergo's talents behind a grill, it would allow the little diner to expand to a full-service basement rib restaurant.

The ribs are famous, and famous people eat them. Presidents eat them. The King ate them. Killer eats them. The Rolling Stones. Even NSYNC. They even eat them when they're not in Memphis. And so can you. Go to the restaurant's web site at www.hogsfly.com (get it?), where they tell you all about the extra special care they take in shipping their ribs to you. You can order them today and eat them tomorrow! Cool!

Rendezvous is located at 52 South Second Street.

CORKY'S BBQ • MEMPHIS

It all started in Memphis. Corky's BBQ opened in 1984 as a small cozy place with wood walls and lots of neon lights and polished brass. Wait staff in bow ties and white shirts. Music from the 1950s and 1960s rocks the joint. Founder Don Pelts had envisioned this restaurant since the early 1970s, so he had plenty of time to perfect it.

He had plenty of time to perfect his ribs, too. They're cooked Memphis-style, the old fashioned way—slow cooked over hickory and charcoal and hand pulled only. He must be doin' somethin' right, for Corky's has been voted number one

Eat, Drink, and Be Merry!

in Memphis for eighteen years straight. It's also been featured on cable television's Food Network and *Bon Apetite* and *Southern Living* magazines.

The restaurant is so popular that it has multiplied like little piggies on a farm. You'll find Corky's in ten states, including as fur north as the Yankee states of Illinois and Indiana. And it all started in Memphis.

Corky's BBQ has been voted number one in Memphis for almost two decades straight.
Courtesy of Corky's BBQ.

Located at 5259 Popular Avenue.

ERNESTINE AND HAZEL'S • NASHVILLE

This old-time juke joint was once a wh...brothel! And the steamy ghost of its past lingers in every creaky floorboard and dirty window. Paint peels from the walls and the stairs threaten to give way as you make your way up to the old cathouse rooms—now turned into private lounges.

Popular with the locals, Ernestine and Hazel's is a great place to jam. Downstairs, the main bar has a dance floor jumping to the funk-filled jukebox. Upstairs, with a little quiet, you can enjoy live jazz piano.

You can't get cocktails here, just beer. And the only food available is Ernestine and Hazel's famous Soul Burger, slathered with their secret soul sauce. It's enough.

Located at 531 South Main Street.

A Little Nashville Trivia

1. Nashville was founded on Christmas Eve 1779.
2. Presidents Andrew Jackson and James Polk lived in Nashville.
3. The original name of the *Grand Ole Opry* was the *WSM Barn Dance*.
4. Nashville's Music Row encompasses parts of 16th and 17th Avenue South.
5. Singer Roy Acuff was known as the King of Country.
6. Chet Atkins was known as Mr. Guitar.
7. Country music artist Randy Travis used to wash dishes at the Nashville Palace.
8. Singer Kathy Mattea started out as a tour guide for the Country Music Hall of Fame in Nashville.
9. Bill Monroe was known as the Father of Bluegrass.

Eat, Drink, and Be Merry!

EXIT/IN • NASHVILLE

Maybe if they'd named it something else, this music hall would've had an easier go of it. As it is, the joint has become infamous for its numerous closings and openings in the last thirty years. But, troubled or not, the place has without a doubt played a major role in the history of American music.

Big names have played here since the doors first opened in 1971. Before the stage was even finished, a frizzy-haired guy in cut offs walked in and asked for an

Newly reopened, Exit/In provides Tennessee with an eclectic mix of music.
Courtesy of Exit/In.

audition. He was hired on the spot and became one of Exit/In's hot young acts. The frizzy hair's mostly gone now, but the cut-offs remain. And Jimmy Buffett's music's still got a Caribbean soul that's hard to control and some Tennessee hidden deep in its heart.

Linda Ronstadt did a Mondays-through-Wednesdays gig that first year. Steve Martin honed his act here in those early days as well, often taking the crowd out to wreak havoc on Elliston Place.

The Exit/In's last closing and opening was in 2002, and since that time, it's received a makeover, with a completely revamped sound and light systems. The bands booked include well-known country, rock, and indie bands. No matter who's playing though, a visit there is a visit into music's past.

Located at 2208 Elliston Place.

HUEY'S MIDTOWN • MEMPHIS

Blues, brews, and burgers are what you'll find at Huey's. They're all great, but the burgers might be the best. The restaurant has, in

Huey's has been voted the best burger in town for eighteen years running.
Courtesy of Huey's Midtown.

fact won the Best Burger in Memphis award eighteen years running. There's live music on Sundays.

Located at 1927 Madison Avenue.

LULU GRILLE • MEMPHIS

Some years ago, Don McLean told wife Leigh about his dream for their future: They'd sell all their worldly possessions, buy a sailboat, and sail around the world. She could home, uh, boat school the kids and serve as the galley wench. After she stopped laughing, they set out to make Don's second dream for their future come true.

Eat, Drink, and Be Merry!

And some dreams do come true. Lulu Grille opened in 1991 as what Don and Leigh like the think of as a true "Mom and Pop." The place is named after one daughter, the other daughter, Amanda, has the veranda named for her, and son John, well, not only does he have a whole room named for him, he has a whole wall in there. Course only the guys get to see that wall.

Anyhoo. The menu doesn't scream Mom and Pop. No cheese and crackers here. And you won't find any of those yucky pickled eggs floatin' in red stuff in big old jars either. What you will find are items such as green-lip mussels (OK, that don't sound so good. But it is.), and grilled quail. There is duck in tagliatelle pasta, filet mignon, veal piccata , and shrimp and crab meat penne. Know what that means, right? Yep, ain't no "cook" out there in the kitchen. Naw. They got a real live "chef."

The whole crew seems to be doin' themselves proud. Lulu Grille has been named Best Kept Secret year after year by the readers of *Memphis Magazine*. Bet it beats living on a leaky old boat.

Located at 565 Erin Drive.

Rum Boogie Café • Memphis

OK, you don't wanna miss this juke joint. True to its name, it offers lots of fine rum and some really hot boogie. The food's pretty good too, including ribs, fried catfish, Cajun dishes, and barbecue.

What this club serves up best, though, is some steamy R&B. House favorite James Govan and the Boogie Blues Band rock the nights on a regular basis and more often than not, national acts show up and jam on stage.

If that's not enough, there's a really cool collection of more than 350 guitars to see. They're autographed by the folks who've played

The Rum Boogie Café is famous for its R&B.
Courtesy of Carson Lamm.

there, including Aerosmith, Stevie Ray Vaughn, and the B-52s.

Located at 182 Beale Street.

Ever wonder how your Granny got her cathead biscuits so big and fluffy? We betcha she used Martha White Flour. This Southern staple got its start in 1899, when Richard Lindsey, owner of the Royal Flour Mill named his best flour after his three-year-old daughter.

In 1941, Lindsey sold the company to the Cohen Williams family, who hocked the farm to buy it. Wizards in marketing, they never looked back. It was the Williams family that coined the slogan "Goodness Gracious, It's Good!" The 1945 slogan was a phrase that became synonymous with Martha White for many years.

Knowing their demographic (before that word became so ubiquitous), they sponsored a 5:45 a.m. radio show, *Martha White Biscuit and Cornbread Time*, on Nashville's WSM radio. They expanded their advertising to include the Grand Ole Opry, where they remain the show's longest running sponsor.

The Williamses also knew innovation. In the 1950s, they added Hot Rize, a powerful new secret ingredient that made Mama's job easier and revolutionized baking forever.

Check Granny's cupboard, we'll bet you'll find a box of Martha's Quick and Easy Biscuit Mix right there on the shelf. Lawdy, child. Granny's got the Harley revvin' in the driveway. No time to make those biscuits from scratch!

Miscellaneous Miscellany

It's the Law!

Better watch your step in our Strange But True Tennessee. You never know when the long arm of the law may reach out and nab you for breaking some of these strange but true laws!

1. It's illegal to use a lasso to catch a fish. Com'ere you little sucker. Let me git this hook in your mouth.

2. It's legal to gather and consume road kill. Hey, Grandpa! What's for supper?

3. You can't shoot any game other than whales from a moving automobile. Gotta find 'em first.

4. Stealing a horse is punishable by hanging. Honest, officer. He followed me home!

5. In Fayette County, it's illegal to have more than five inoperable vehicles on one piece of property. And only three of those can be up on blocks.

6. In Lexington, no one may eat ice cream on the sidewalk. Melts too quick there anyway.

7. Driving is not to be done while asleep. But, officer, I just closed my eyes for a moment.

8. In Dyersburg, it's illegal for a woman to call a man. You hussy!

9. More than eight women cannot live in the same house, because it would constitute a brothel. You hussies!

10. It's illegal for frogs to croak after 11 p.m. It's 10:59. Hang on, we wanna watch them enforce this one!

Strange Town Names

It's not just the laws in some of our Tennessee towns that are strange. How about some of the town names? Did you know you could travel the globe without ever leaving the state? Traveling through Tennessee you can visit Asia, Athens, Bogota, Cairo, Camelot, Cuba, Denmark, Denver, Detroit, Egypt, Lebanon, Manila, Mecca, Moscow, Palestine, Paris, Philadelphia, and Rome.

If world travel's not your thing, try these interestingly named towns. There's Backwoods and Barefoot. Bugtussle and Bugscuffle. Frog Jump, Goat City, Owl Hoot, and Polecat. Try out Disco and Hoodoo. Who do? We do.

Here are a few towns and their names we can tell you about.

ALAMO • CROCKETT COUNTY

Alamo? Crockett? Got a clue as to where this town got its name? See, that intrepid frontiersman Davy Crockett may have wondered far and wide in his lifetime, but he started out in Tennessee. Crockett was born near Limestone on the Nolichucky River. And Tennessee is proud of its wondering son.

Alamo began life as Cageville, honoring the fellow who first opened a store on the site. But then the Alamo happened, and Davy was killed. The town was renamed to honor him.

BELL BUCKLE • BEDFORD COUNTY

There are two versions of how this town got its name. One says that a settler's cow got too close to Indian land. It was killed and the collar, which had a bell on it, was attached to a tree by its buckle as a warning.

The other story says that the Indians carved a bell and buckle as a symbol of the cows, which wore collars with bells on them, on a tree as a warning to the settlers to keep their animals closer.

BUCKSNORT • HICKMAN COUNTY

There are two stories as to how this town got its name. One is boring. The other is not. First the boring one: White tail deer proliferate in the area, and it's speculated that the

Bucksnort was named after a moonshiner.
Courtesy of Bucksnort.

town is named for the snorting sound of a buck around the Sugar Creek area.

Now the fun one. We're going with this one. Seems there was a moonshiner named Buck living in the area. Those making purchases from Buck told others they were going to Buck's for a snort, which, especially after a snort or two, got shortened to Buck's snort then to Bucksnort.

CHATTANOOGA • HAMILTON COUNTY

Chattanooga means "rock coming to a point" in the Creek Indian language, referring, most believe, to Lookout Mountain.

A view from Lookout Mountain.
Courtesy of Chattanooga CVB.

GRABALL• CARROLL COUNTY

According to legend, this community got its name when some local residents were engaged in some type of unspecified questionable activity—a card game or chicken fight, say— when the Sheriff showed up. Someone shouted "Grab all you can and run!"

Lick Skillet • Decatur County

Supposedly this town was named by a bunch of campers. Seems that in the early days, before highways and motels on every corner, there was a lot of camping along the roadsides. One night, a group of campers cooked a big meal, but one late feller got left out. Finding no food left, he licked the skillet, and ever after the town was called Lick Skillet.

Skullbone • Gibson County

This was—maybe still is—a rough and tumble little community, known for the bare-knuckle fighting matches once held there. These matches were called skullboning. And that's how the town got its name.

Stinking Creek • Campbell County

What a nasty name for such a pretty area. Seems that the winter of 1779 was frightfully cold. Snow began in late October and intense cold followed for weeks. The streams froze over and animals dropped left and right, where they were frozen—until spring.

Beautiful warm weather returned, but for months afterward Indian and white hunters alike avoided the area because of the stench of rotting animal flesh. The buzzards loved it! Anyway, the stench went away, but the name stuck.

Suck Creek • Marion County

This little community is named for the nearby creek that runs into the Tennessee River. It's called Suck Creek because as it flows into the river, it causes rapids and whirlpools that have been known to suck in boats.

Miscellaneous Miscellany

Suck-Egg Hollow

There's a rumor about a small community in Tennessee with this name, which it got from a trigger-happy chicken farmer. The farmer's eggs were being eaten by some unidentified animal, so the farmer just shot any animal that came around. He finally learned it was black snakes sucking eggs.

Sweet Lips • Chester County

So named for the Civil War soldiers who stopped for a swig at the nearby stream.

Wartburg • Morgan County

Well, when we heard this one, we thought the town may have had a problem with incontinent frogs, but that was not the case. When the settlers from Germany and Switzerland saw the terrain of this area, it reminded them of the Thuringia area around Germany, where the Wartburg Castle lies. Homesick, perhaps, they named the area for the castle. Hmm…too bad the castle wasn't named a purtier name.

Plans are in the works to build a full-scale replica of Wartburg Castle here.

Towns of Note

BRISTOL • SULLIVAN COUNTY

Bet you thought Nashville was the Birthplace of Country Music. Nah. That little ol' city's just a pretender to the throne. Bristol is the official Birthplace of Country Music, so designated by no less than the U.S. Congress.

The roots of country music lie in the music the Southern Appalachian settlers brought with them in the 1700s. New influences came here as well with traveling vaudeville and medicine shows. The native fiddle of the English, Scotch, and Irish and the banjo of African origin found their way here, and after World War II, the guitar, auto harp, and dulcimer were added.

Ralph Peer, a pioneer in the music industry, recognized the untapped market for rural mountain music, and with the advent of portable recording, he set up a base of operations in Bristol—a town divided, by the way. Half of the town lies in Tennessee and half lies in Virginia. Each half has its own government and city services. Peer chose Bristol because of its proximity to local talent, such as Earnest and Hattie Stoneman, The Johnson Brothers, and Henry Whitter.

Soon, talent from other states, particularly the Carter Family from Virginia and Jimmie Rodgers from North Carolina, came to Bristol to be recorded. It was these "Bristol Sessions," that gave birth to country music.

In 1998, the United States Congress passed a resolution recognizing Bristol as the Birthplace of Country Music and in the mid-1990s, the Birthplace of Country Music Alliance (BCMA) was founded in Bristol to promote and support the music traditions of the area.

CHATTANOOGA • HAMILTON COUNTY

Yeah, we know Chattanooga's got a lot of noted stuff, but nothing beats this! Chattanooga is the birthplace of a hallowed Southern tradition—the MoonPie and R.C. Cola. According to historian Ronald Dickson in his book *The Great American MoonPie Handbook*, the custom got its start in 1917, when Earl Mitchell Sr., a

Tourists enjoy the view from Chattanooga's pier.
Courtesy of Chattanooga CVB.

salesman for the Chattanooga Bakery, quizzed miners on what they might enjoy for a snack. The miners replied they wanted something for their lunch pails, something solid and filling. Mitchell asked them about how big they wanted this snack.

Well, sir, the big ol' Southern moon was coming out right about then, and one of the miners held out his hands, framed the moon, and said, "About that big." With that in mind

Mitchell returned to the bakery, where he noticed some workers dipping graham cookies in marshmallow and placing them on the window sill to harden. Another cookie was added then a coating of chocolate, and voila! A tradition is born.

By the 1950s, the MoonPie had become so popular that the Chattanooga Bakery didn't have the resources to make anything else. It was in the 1950s that the MoonPie was paired with R.C. (Royal Crown) Cola. Back then you could buy a special for 10 cents—16 ounces of R.C. and a MoonPie weighing in at around half a pound. The combination has been celebrated in song and print and still finds its way into any red-blooded Southerner's diet.

ELIZABETHTON • CARTER COUNTY

The first constitution ever drafted by a white man in America was written in Elizabethton in 1772. It was patterned after the constitution of the Iroquois League of Nations, a federal system of government developed more than two hundred years before for five eastern Native American tribes.

GREENEVILLE • GREENE COUNTY

Daaavvyy, Davy Crockett! King of the Wild Frontier! Yep, Davy Crockett, he was our hero. Funny thing, though, he looked a lot like Dan'el Boone back then, didn't he?

Anyway, he weren't born on a mountaintop in Tennessee as that song says. But he was born in Tennessee, near Greenville, where a replica of his log cabin stands today.

Miscellaneous Miscellany

Grinder's Switch • Centerville, Hickman County

The town of Grinder's Switch was the imaginary hometown of Miss Minnie Pearl, the character created by Centerville native Sarah Ophelia Colley. She appropriated the town name from an actual railroad junction, located across the Duck River from the Colleytown area of Centerville where she grew up.

Colley portrayed the man-chasing Minnie Pearl for more than fifty years, starting out on the *Grand Ole Opry* with a three-minute gig on November 30, 1940. The spot was wildly popular and Colley, an aspiring actress, developed the country-bumpkin character, complete with homespun gingham dress, white cotton stockings, Mary Janes, and most memorable of all, a straw hat bedecked with silk flowers and dangling a price tag of $1.98. She always walked on stage with a loud "How-dee!"

To all those who knew her, she had little in common with Minnie Pearl. A graduate of a fashionable finishing school in Nashville, she was gracious, soft-spoken, and always well dressed—old gentrified Nashville personified.

Colley once said of Grinder's Switch: "As I grow older, the place is no longer an abandoned loading dock in Hickman County. Grinder's Switch is a state of mind—a place where there is no illness, no war, no unhappiness—where all you worry about is what you're going to wear to the church social, and if your feller is going to kiss you in the moonlight on the way home. I wish you all a Grinder's Switch."

After she died in 1996, her hometown and county honored her (and developed a purt good tourist attraction) by developing the Grinder's Switch Center, where you'll find

Minnie Pearl memorabilia and can view some of her performances.

Located at 209 East Public Square.

Jonesborough • Washington County

Jonesborough is the oldest town in Tennessee. Founded in 1779, the town was originally part of the Lost State of Franklin, a portion of North Carolina that incorporated into a full-fledged state.

The folks in the western area of North Carolina were quite unhappy with the treatment they were getting from the state, with taxation being a particular rub. In 1785, things finally

Jonesborough was founded in 1779, making it Tennessee's oldest town.
Courtesy of Frank Young, Lasting Impressions, Boone, NC.

came to a head and the folks of what's now East Tennessee started their own state. They wrote to Benjamin Franklin, asking for permission to name their state after him, and inviting him to come live there. Tennessee native John Sevier stepped up to serve as governor.

The state, however, was plagued by intrigue and was

constantly harassed by the Cherokee and by North Carolina—which was a big part of the state's downfall. While Sevier was off fighting the Cherokee, North Carolina seized his land for taxes they said he owed them.

In February 1788, Seiver laid siege upon John Tipton, a powerful North Carolina citizen, in an attempt to regain his land. Unfortunately for him—and the state of Franklin—men on both sides were neighbors and friends. They didn't want to kill each other. So, most deliberately missed their shots and the battle just kinda played itself out with few men injured. Known as The Battle for the Lost State of Franklin, this battle was the beginning of the end for the fledging state. Within the year, Franklin collapsed. Sevier went on to serve office in North Carolina and Franklin became East Tennessee.

Lebanon • Wilson

Way back in the 1960s, Dan Evins was working in the family gasoline business and began thinking of ways to meet the needs of the people on the road. Dan thought that, though fast food might be a good business idea, it sure weren't very good eatin'.

What folks on the road needed, he decided, was a place they could get good country food, with everything—from mashed taters to biscuits to turnip greens—made from scratch. Plus, there needed to be an old country store like in the good old days, warmed by a pot-bellied stove and filled with big jars of candy and homemade jellies.

So, Evins built the first Cracker Barrel Old Country Store, and his thinking proved quite sound. That one store multiplied to thirteen in 1977. Between 1980 and 1990, eighty-four stores opened across the country and by 1996 there were 260 Cracker Barrels.

Today, there are 540 stores in forty-one states. Evins still runs the business under the same principle as always. He says the goal isn't to simply recreate a time gone by. It's to preserve it, because the lifestyle of rural American isn't about where you live. It's about how you live.

LYNCHBURG • MOORE

Lynchburg, Jack Daniel. Jack Daniel, Lynchburg. For millions throughout the civilized world, if you hear one you hear the other, and either can conjure the taste of the South, shady verandas, honey suckle breezes, and good sippin' whiskey.

Jack Daniel began the whiskey-making business at an early age. He was just seven when he was hired out to work with the Dan Call family. Call was a Lutheran minister who also ran a whiskey still on the Louse River. Daniel learned all about whiskey and how mellowing it through charcoal gave it a unique flavor. He was only thirteen when Call, hearing a stronger call to the ministry, sold his still to Daniel.

By 1866, Daniel had perfected his charcoal mellowing process and had registered his distillery, being the first in the nation to do so and making it the oldest registered distillery in the country.

Miscellaneous Miscellany

NUTBUSH • HAYWOOD COUNTY

Nutbush City Limits. That's where Anna Mae Bullock, a.k.a. Tina Turner, grew up. Of African-American and Navajo descent, Turner first became known for her fiery 1960s and 1970s performances with the Ike and Tina Turner Revue. One of the hottest songs in the revue was the song written by Tina that told the story of her hometown, "Nut Bush City Limits." The song made the little "one-horse town" where you "have to be careful what you're puttin' down," internationally known.

Tina Turner made the small town of Nutbush famous with her song "Nut Bush City Limits." Courtesy of Thomas R Machnitzki.

Undoubtedly, Turner's upbringing played a role in both her relationship with Ike, a relationship that became famously abusive, and her phenomenal comeback in the 1980s as a solo act, wild-haired, long-legged, and big-voiced.

SHELBYVILLE • SHELBY COUNTY

Shelbyville has two titles to claim. The city is the Walking Horse Capital of the World and is known as the Pencil City because of its historical importance to pencil manufacturing. It's the birthplace of the Sharpie, the largest selling writing instrument, produced by the Sanford Corporation.

But Shelbyville is better known for the horses. It's here

that the Cadillac of the horse world was first "built." It began back in the early 1800s, when the plantation owners were looking for a horse that could handle the mountainous terrain. Breeders blended the Narragansett Pacer and the Canadian Pacer. During the Civil War, they added a drop or two of Confederate Pacer and a smattering of the Union Trotter and came up with the sturdy Southern Plantation Horse. To refine the breed, they added Thoroughbred, Standardbred, Morgan, and American Saddlebred.

In 1885, Black Allen, the foundation sire of the new Tennessee Walking Horse breed, was born. The breed quickly became popular because of its incredible stamina and for its smooth, swinging gait that was easy on the rider's derriere. If you've ever ridden one, you'd know; it's like riding a Cadillac.

Today, Shelbyville is still the center of the Tennessee Walking Horse industry, with more horses per capita in Shelby County than anywhere else in the world. The Grand Champion Tennessee Walking Horse is crowned in Shelbyville every year at the Tennessee Walking Horse Celebration.

Funny Happenings Here

Motorcycle mamas, boats on parade, tall tale tellin'…There's funny happenings going on in Strange But True Tennessee.

BELL'S & BENGE'S MEMORIAL MOTORCYCLE RIDE & AMERICAN INDIAN SOCIAL & REENACTMENT WALK FESTIVAL • GILES COUNTY

Wondering just who Bell and Benge were? Well, we're gonna tell ya. It all has to do with the Indian Removal Act, which relocated more than one hundred thousand Native Americans from across the Southeast. The act was passed in 1830 with Tennesseean Andrew Jackson as president. Tennessee congressman Davy Crockett strongly opposed the bill, but it passed by just one vote. This removal was accomplished by forcing the Indians to travel by four main routes. More than four thousand died on the journey. The Cherokee called it "Nunna dual Isuny," which means "The Trail Where We Cried."

Two of the land routes, the one led by John Benge and the more southern route led by John Bell, passed through Giles County, making it the only location in the U.S. to have a connection to more than one land route. The annual motorcycle ride was organized as a fitting memorial to those who died on the Trial of Tears and to Davy Crockett for his strong opposition to the Act.

Funny Happenings Here

Don't let them kid you, though, the main thing is that it's a good excuse for motorcyclists to jump astride their steel horses and feel the wind in their faces. For those of you who haven't discovered that life is more exciting when you're barreling through it astride 750 pounds of steel, there's a reenactment of the Trail of Tears walk. The ride and walk converge in Pulaski at the Trail of Tears Interpretive Center, where there's a special presentation for the riders. A Native American social follows.

BLACKBERRY FESTIVAL • LYNNVILLE

Held in June, this celebration of the blackberry includes music and dancing. There's a carnival and a horse show and, of course, there are blackberry treats everywhere. Don't miss your taste of the World's Biggest Blackberry Pie!

BONNAROO MUSIC FESTIVAL • MANCHESTER

Think Woodstock twenty-five years later. There's quite some resemblance to be found in this wild party of a music festival. It, too, is held in a cow pasture—seven hundred picturesque acres in Manchester. There's mud. There's heat. A lack of hygiene. Kids running around in next to nothing. The smell of strange herbs in the air. The general feel is the same: Bonnaroo has been voted Festival of the Year by the most prestigious music magazines. *Rolling Stone* called it "one of the 50 moments to change the history of rock and roll" and the *New York Times* said it has revolutionized the modern rock festival. Groovy! Oh, we mean Phat! No, wait, the '60s are back. Groovy!

The array of bands appearing in the Bonnaroo—which is

Bonnaroo is an annual music festival in Manchester, Tennessee.
Used with permission of Bonnaroo.com.

Creole slang for "good times," by the way—is staggering. Every genre is represented, from old-time country to indie-rock, from funk to punk to reggae. No matter what your taste in music, you'll find plenty to groove on. And you don't have to leave civilization behind. The festival features a cow-pasture city, complete with the largest wireless internet deployment in the U.S. Hey, man, we gotta stay wired!

CANJOE MUSIC SESSIONS • BLOUNTVILLE

Next time you're visiting Blountville, check to see if the CanJoe Company is hosting one of its music sessions, featuring rock, country, bluegrass, and blues, and, oh, yeah, canjoe music. Never heard of canjoe music? Well, ya just don't know what you've missed.

The canjoe was first developed by North Carolinian Herschel Brown, who got the idea from a Uni-Can instrument he discovered in his mountain travels. It's recycling at its best. It's a one-stringed instrument, with metal frets and a soda can.

Funny Happenings Here

Yes, you heard right, a soda can is used as the belly of the instrument. Brown found the twelve-ounce soda cans had a better sound than your garden-variety dog food can, which was the can of choice in the Uni-Can.

Brown's modern canjoe is comprised of a slender wood fingerboard with ten frets, a single tuner key, and one string pulled through a beverage or food can. It's picked like a one-stringed guitar.

The Canjoe is now being manufactured by John VanArsdall, aka CanJoe John, whom Brown chose as a successor after hearing Van Arsdall's fiddle playing. CanJoe John performs at festivals and concerts around the country. He also has released a couple of CDs. His first "One String, One Can, One Man, One Band..." he says "has been played on radio stations around the world." His second CD, "An Uncanny Christmas," is another don't-miss.

CanJoe John says the canjoe is an instrument that anyone can play, "even if you can't carry a tune in a bucket or play the radio." His instruments are expertly crafted using carefully selected materials. And, he'll do everything he can to fill special orders for brand-name cans. (Think he could find one a

According to CanJoe John, anyone can learn to play the canjoe. Courtesy of CanJoe John.

them Billy Beer cans?) The premium, limited edition, and very limited editions are reserved for lovers of fine art. They are crafted from fine hard and exotic woods and rare collectable cans. With the very limited editions, the cans are personally autographed by CanJoe John.

There's a hairy creature inhabiting the forests and swamps of Tennessee, and no it's not your Uncle Buddy off on a toot. Might be Aunt Thelma, though. This creature is about seven feet tall, is sheepdog hairy, and has a face that would stop a clock. Got big feet, too. Wears about a size 52. Yep, that's Auntie T, all right.

All (well, most) kidding aside, that tall, dark, and hairy guy that many people think inhabits only the far away Pacific Northwest is quite a popular feller around the South. He's made so many appearances, in fact, that quite a few groups have formed to record and document sightings. The Gulf Coast Bigfoot Research Organization is one of such groups. They maintain a database of Bigfoot sightings across the Southeast.

CLINCH MOUNTAIN MUSICFEST • KINGSPORT

Old-timey music. Hillbilly music. Appalachian music. No matter what you call it, the music of the mountains sings in the soul of America. The songs tell the stories of a people and a heritage.

Funny Happenings Here

Because of the isolation of the southern Appalachian settlements, mountain music did not change much over hundreds of years. It's known for its instrumental tradition, particularly instruments such as the mountain dulcimer, fiddle, banjo, and the limberjack, a wooden doll used as a percussion instrument. The ballads told stories, covering every area of mountain life, including tragedy, happiness, humor, religion, heroism, and the supernatural.

The Clinch Mountain MusicFest is dedicated to preserving the old-time music and the heritage of the mountains for future generations. Each year they share the unique music and inspire others in the ways of the strong mountain people who, through their songs, have shaped our country.

COLONIAL FAIR • GOODLETTSVILLE

This affair has become nationally known in recent years as one of the country's best re-creation events. Named to the Top 20 Events in the Southeast by the Southeast Tourism Society, the festival features a cast of more than six hundred costumed participants in a re-creation of an eighteenth century fair.

Held in the Moss-Wright Park, the fair's picturesque setting meanders around Mansker's Station, a recreation of an eighteenth century travel station and the original Bowen Plantation House, Goodlettsville's earliest residence. More than one hundred merchant traders and folk artisans and craftsmen offer their wares for household and camp. With two stages and some more intimate musical settings located within Bowen House, entertainment is almost continuous. Food representative of the period is offered in several tented pubs. There's Scottish dancing and puppeteers, and be on guard for a peek at the wild side of eighteenth century life, with beggars, trollops, pickpockets, preachers, and Indians wandering around.

Held annually in May.

COVERED BRIDGE CELEBRATION • ELIZABETHTON

The Doe River Covered Bridge is one of only four covered bridges remaining in Tennessee. Every year, the town celebrates the beauty and heritage of the covered bridge with a four-day festival of arts and crafts, music

The Covered Bridge Celebration is held annually in Elizabethton.
Courtesy of Elizabethton Chamber of Commerce.

with nightly entertainment, dancing, and kids' activities.

Held annually in June.

CRAPE MYRTLE FESTIVAL • ARDMORE

Much of the South is Asian. If that statement is confusing, consider the fact that kudzu, that ubiquitous climbing vine, came to us from Japan in 1876. Since that time, kudzu has proliferated.

Funny Happenings Here

Consider, then, that the South's most popular flowering tree, the Crape Myrtle, came to us from Asia as well—although it was a Frenchie that first introduced it. Andre Michaux was a

It's murder most foul. Every year, thousands of horticulturists and homeowners across the South commit a heinous act on the South's most popular flowering tree. For reasons authorities find completely mysterious, these fine upstanding citizens commit Crape Murder. With pruning shears as murder weapons, at the end of blooming season every year they cruelly hack off the limbs of the tree, leaving nothing but a bunch of stubs. It's a horrible, horrible crime!

According to horticulture expert Greg Grant, this butchering act leaves nasty permanent scars and wounds. It results in a Crape Myrtle that's deformed, with skinny, out-of-proportion limbs that aren't strong enough to support the tree's big blooms. No doubt, you've noticed trees whose blooms flop over? It's unattractive, and no doubt painful for the tree. And it's all a result of Crape Murder!

Grant's plea is the same as other experts across the South—stop the madness! Maiming the tree, he says, serves no purpose, so just stop it. Step away from the pruning shears! Let the tree grow! Let it bloom! Case closed. Now, if somebody could only solve that name-spelling mystery...

French botanist, who was sent here by the French government to establish nurseries to cultivate plants for naturalization in France. It was he who introduced the Crape Myrtle tree—in South Carolina—in 1786. Before long, it had found its way into every yard and garden club throughout the South.

The good folks of Ardmore celebrate the Crape Myrtle with an annual festival. There are arts and crafts of all kinds, kids' games, puppet shows, food and live entertainment.

Held the last Saturday in August.

DIANA SINGING • DIANA

The Diana Singing began in 1969 with a conversation about an all night singing being held in Nashville at the Ryman Auditorium. It suddenly hit the two fellers discussing it that, hey, if folks would go to Nashville to hear singing all night, might they also come to Diana to sing all night?

The two spent $15 to have cards printed up for advertising, and they began touting their idea around town. Their enthusiasm for the

Diana Singing is a biannual, night long singing festival held twice a year in this hay shed.
Courtesy of Randy Jenkins.

project was contagious and their theory was proved correct: Hundreds of people showed up at the Diana Church of Christ to participate in that first all-night singing.

Each year it grew bigger, each year the church had to find a bigger place to accommodate more singing folks. Finally, they built a hay shed especially for the purpose. Today, more than three thousand attend the twice-yearly singings.

Held biannually in June and September.

DOLLYWOOD • PIGEON FORGE

We weren't even gonna mention Dollywood, because, frankly, it's come to resemble that monstrous park further South. You know—the one that houses the mouse that ate Florida. But then, we took a few moments to remember the history of this park, and we knew we had to add it. Besides, anything named "Dollywood" has to be strange but true!

Dollywood started out in 1961 as a small Civil War-themed tourist attraction called Rebel Railroad. A couple of name changes and new owners later, it was bought by

Dollywood is Tennessee's number one tourist attraction.
Courtesy of Dollywood.

Dolly Parton and changed to, what else, Dollywood, in 1986. Today, Dollywood's Smoky Mountain Adventure is Tennessee's number one attraction. One hundred and thirty acres of incredible rides! Spectacular shows! Heritage crafts! Fun for the whole family!

Located 1020 Dollywood Lane.

FARM MACHINERY SHOW • GILES COUNTY

Oh, what fun! Well, actually, it is fun. Yeah, you can look at lots of farm machinery if you want. There is some pretty cool antique machinery. There are arts, crafts, and food. The really fun part comes with the games, such as the slow tractor race and the children's tractor races.

GOBBLER GALA • GILES COUNTY

A county-wide event, the Gobbler Gala features live music and lots of fun. You can feast on such delectable treats as turkey dogs and turkey burgers, finished off with fried pies for dessert.

GREAT PUMPKIN FESTIVAL AND WEIGH OFF • ALLARDT

Good grief, Charlie Brown! The Great Pumpkin does exist! And he's throwing a heck of a party in Allardt! There are music in the park, a decorating contest, a Pumpkin Beauty Contest (no, the winner is not round and orange!), a Great Pumpkin Festival King and Queen, a 5K Pumpkin Run (didn't know they had legs), and a Pumpkin Weigh-off. And that's just the first day!

Don't miss the Pumpkin Festival Parade, the car show, the motorcycle show, the costume contest, bake sale and silent auction, recipe contest, and a talent show! Whew! We're not through! There also the Mayberry Memories, where Gomer and other cast members bring the Mayberry Squad Car and sign autographs! Shazaam! Music! Crafts! Food!

Wow! Linus knew it all along.

Held in annually in October.

INTERNATIONAL DOGWOOD FESTIVAL • WINCHESTER

A tree that rivals the Crape Myrtle for popularity and ubiquity in the South is the Dogwood tree. This gnarly little tree grows wild throughout the South and is a popular landscape tree.

Tennessee produces more dogwoods than any other state, and Franklin County, with the good luck to be situated in two growing zones, has a well-established dogwood industry. In the 1800s, Franklin County nurserymen developed many new varieties, called "cultivars," including the first red variety, the Cherokee Chief.

To celebrate the dogwood and its place in Franklin County history, the city of Winchester hosts the annual International

The beautiful dogwood tree has inspired many legends as well as Tennessee's International Dogwood Festival.
Courtesy of the city of Winchester.

Dogwood Festival. The festival is jam packed with things to do, including live entertainment from country, rock, and gospel artists, arts and crafts, horse-drawn buggy rides, a weight-lifting contest, a flower show, a tour of area historic homes, food, a 5K run, and more.

In its short history, the festival has quickly become a winner, literally. In 2005, the International Festivals and Events Association named the city of Winchester and its International Dogwood Festival as an award winner. The festival was chosen from a field of fifteen hundred national and international contestants. In 2004, its first year, the festival also was given one silver and four bronze awards.

The festival is held annually in April.

The Jack Daniel Distillery Tour • Lynchburg

There are folks that take this tour on a yearly basis. Not sure why. The distillery is in a dry county, so ya don't get to sample the wares. Maybe it's that fermentin' room. You might get a buzz there from the scent of all that Jack Daniel's whiskey fermenting!

Expect to leave with a head full of knowledge, but no whiskey at the Jack Daniel Distillery.
Courtesy of Jack Daniel's.

The guided tour is free and it takes about two hours, as you weave in and out of warehouses and building on about nine acres of land. There're eighteen different stops, with a story at each one.

Even if you're not a whiskey drinker, the tour is fun and interesting. And, hey, it's well worth the price!

MAD ANTHONY WAYNE DAY • COLLINWOOD

Despite the nickname, Mad Anthony Wayne, for whom Wayne County was named, was a noted general in the American Revolution. Fearless in battle, he stormed his way through the Revolution, becoming one of Washington's most prized generals.

Wayne's nickname came from a neighbor of his, a scoundrel known as Jemmy the Rover because of his frequent desertions from the Army. When Wayne failed to intercede on Jemmy's behalf, the

Mad Anthony Wayne was a general in the American Revolution.
Courtesy of Wikipedia.org.

Rover supposedly remarked, "Anthony is mad. Mad Anthony, that's what he is. Mad Anthony Wayne." This nickname stuck with Wayne, mainly because of his daring and fearless attitude.

Collinwood celebrates ol' Mad Anthony with a heckuva festival every year. There's music and dancing and lots of food, arts and crafts, games, and an antique car and tractor show. The highlight of the festival is the Tour de Wayne bicycle ride, which tours the Natchez Trace and Wayne County.

Held annually in June.

NATIONAL CORNBREAD FESTIVAL • SOUTH PITTSBURG

If ever there were a worthy cause to close down the streets of a city, this is it. For two days every year, South Pittsburg closes the streets of the town's historic district and celebrates one of the South's best loved traditions: good ol' cornbread.

Cooks from all over the country flock to the town to compete in the National Cornbread Championship. There are just two requirements: Your cornbread must be made with the Southern favorite, Martha White cornmeal, and has to be baked in a Lodge cast iron skillet. Umm...umm...Good eating!

In addition to the cook-off, there's a whole weekend of fun, including thrilling rides, artisans practicing their crafts, music, puppeteers, clowns, magicians, ventriloquists. It's a good time for all.

Funny Happenings Here

National Storytelling Festival • Jonesborough

It all started more than thirty years ago. High school journalism teacher Jerry Smith and a carload of students were listening to the *Grand Ole Opry* when humorist and consummate storyteller Jerry Clower told a hilarious story about coon hunting in his home state of Mississippi. It was serendipity.

The International Storytelling Center is located in Jonesborough.
Courtesy of the Historic Jonesborough Visitors Center.

Why not? Inquired Smith. Why not have a storytelling festival right there in Northeast Tennessee? Well, suh, that's just what Smith did. He organized the first National Storytelling Festival. He set up hay bales and wagons for stages and passed the word.

On a warm October weekend in 1973, fewer than sixty people—audience and storytellers—attended, but it was clear that a new tradition was born. The little Tennessee town would be forever changed.

More than thirty years later, the festival is acclaimed as one of the Top 100 Events in North America. Storytellers from all over the world gather here to spin their tales of humor, drama, and everyday life. The hay bales and wagons have been replaced with circus tents and the audience these days number in the thousands.

The National Storytelling Festival is the oldest and most respected gathering devoted to storytelling. It is credited with spawning a renewed interest in the art and has sparked a national revival.

PETERS HOLLOW EGG FIGHT • ELIZABETHTON

When we first heard about this, we figured the folks of Elizabethton had egg on their faces, but not so! The Peters Hollow Egg Fight is a tradition that started way back in 1823 as a little Sunday afternoon rivalry between chicken farmers in Peters Hollow and Rome Hollow. It's not the kinda fight you might think, though. This fight is to determine who has the hardest eggs.

Each competitor cups an egg in a hand. They then tap their eggs together, end on end until one cracks. The competitor whose egg cracks, hands over his egg to the other and it's placed in a basket, no longer to be used. The fight progresses up and down the hollow, the audience in close pursuit. One by one, the competitors run short of eggs and fall by the wayside, until the last two competitors are left. Whoever has the last uncracked egg is the champion. He gets bragging rights for the year.

Contestants can enter up to six dozen eggs—chicken eggs, only—and the folks of Peters Hollow are serious about competition. All year long, they work to improve their chances of winning, with such experiments as adding oyster shells to their chicken feed and breeding species of chickens that lay harder eggs.

You're invited to join in the festivities, too. You'll be welcomed, and don't worry about being an outsider—the folks of Elizabethton are good eggs. Oh, come on. You knew we couldn't resist.

PIE BIRD CONVENTION • PARIS

Paris, Tennessee, is a hot bed, we tell you. A hotbed of pie birds and pie bird activity. Don't know what a pie bird is? Ha! We do. A pie bird is a useful little item to have if you like baking pies. You see, it's a hollow china or ceramic figure, most often in the shape of a bird. Ranging in size from three to five inches, it's placed in the center of the unbaked crust and the pie filling is poured around it. As the pie bakes, the juices are vented into the hollow of the pie bird, keeping the pie from boiling over in the oven and the crust from getting soggy. Cool, huh?

There are lots of folks who think so. They collect pie birds, as a matter of fact. Not only that, but they also travel all around showing off their collections and meeting with other pie bird collectors to discuss pie bird stuff, we guess.

One of the premier gathering places for pie bird collectors is Paris. And there's a reason for that. You see, one of the largest collectors lives right here in little Paris. Linda Fields's collection exceeds fourteen hundred pie birds. She's been featured on television and radio shows and it was her idea to organize a pie bird convention.

RAMP FESTIVAL • COSBY

A two-day festival celebrating ramps? Really, what's one to do? Roll up and down them? Oh, hang on. Not that kind of ramp.

For the uninitiated, the ramp is an onion-like vegetable that was a common spring staple in the Appalachian region of southern Tennessee. The wild growing plant tastes like an onion with a bit of garlic thrown in, and back in the olden days it was believed to have healing powers. It was used as a spring revitalizing tonic. There's just the one thing: The plant's odor is so pungent that it'll make your dog sneeze and your cat run away.

Despite that one little drawback, when the Cosby locals were looking for a gimmick to bring more folks into the area, they quickly voted in a festival honoring the "sweetest tasting and vilest smelling plant in Mother Nature's Bounty." They proved to be savvy in the ways of tourism.

Their first two-day festival, held in 1954, brought in a crowd of approximately six thousand. Why, even the governor showed up. And it just got better from there. In 1955, President Harry Truman attended. In 1959, attendance hit thirty thousand, due mainly to the appearance of Tennessee Ernie Ford, national television celebrity and Bristol native. Other celebrities have stopped by through the years: Eddie Arnold, Roy Acuff, Bill Monroe, Minnie Pearl, Brenda Lee, and Dinah Shore. And they all left in a waft of ramp!

Funny Happenings Here

Today the Ramp Festival is much the same as it was back then, filled with bountiful food, music, dancing, politicians, and the crowning of the Maid of Ramps. Now that's a title you want on your beauty resume, eh? Guess it beats being the Pig Queen.

R.C. Cola and MoonPie Craft Fair • Bell Buckle

This little festival celebrates one of the South's finest traditions: The R.C. Cola and MoonPie. There's the MoonPie Song Contest,

R.C. Cola and MoonPie make a cute couple at the R.C. Cola and MoonPie Festival in Bell Buckle. Courtesy of the city of Bell Buckle.

MoonPie Madness, a ten-mile race, arts and crafts, live music, lots of food (guess what?), and entertainment.

Held in June.

Secret City Festival • Oak Ridge

Oak Ridge is a city born of war. It was established in secrecy and for more than seven years, it didn't exist. It wasn't shown on any maps, no visitors were allowed without special approval, there were guards posted all around, and all citizens were required to wear badges when outside of their homes. Here's the kicker—the city grew to a population of seventy-five thousand and was the fifth largest city in Tennessee. But, shh! It wasn't really there!

The Secret City Festival is held annually in Oak Ridge.
Courtesy of the Oak Ridge Chamber of Commerce.

Why all the secrecy? It all happened when Albert Einstein wrote a letter to President Roosevelt telling him he really needed to get on the ball about this atomic bomb thing. Roosevelt took those words to heart and this nation jumped headlong into the race to create atomic weapons. The Manhattan Project was born.

Tennessee was chosen as a major site for the project for its proximity to the new dam at Norris for easy access to electrical power, the availability of labor in nearby Knoxville, and the sparse population. Another important consideration was the lay of the land, with its valley for the plants and ridges that would contain any accidental explosions. Ooops! The three thousand citizens of Scarboro, New Hope, Robertsville, Elza, and Wheat were given just a matter of weeks to pack up all their possessions and get out.

To accommodate all the people involved at the Tennessee site, which would be searching for the best method of extracting uranium and plutonium, the Corps of Engineers built themselves a city, using prefabricated modular homes, apartments, and dormitories. The town was quickly erected and by 1945, population had swelled to seventy-five thousand. The K-25 uranium-separating facility alone covered forty-four acres, making it the largest building in the world at the time. But, shh! Don't tell anyone!

The secret lasted until after the war. The name of the city was changed to Oak Ridge in 1945—the year the fruit of its labor was dropped on Hiroshima—and it was shifted to civilian control under the authority of Atomic Energy Commission. Then, in 1959 it was incorporated and a city manager and City Council form of government was adopted, moving away from federal control.

The folks of Oak Ridge are proud of the role their city played in history. The purpose of the Secret City Festival, they say, is to promote the history of the city and unite its World War II heritage with the technological advancements ongoing in the city. Sure. We say it's a reason to have some fun.

The theme of the festival leans heavily toward WWII— with reenactments of major battles and a parade of WWII vehicles. But there's also a rock climbing wall, a petting zoo, and arts and crafts. An interactive program at the Children's Museum of Oak Ridge also offers an exhibit entitled Difficult

Decisions, which examines the decisions that led to the dropping of the atomic bomb.

The festival was named one of the Top 25 Summer Activities by *Knoxville* magazine. We'd say the secret's out. And, hey, if you look close enough, we'll bet you can find Oak Ridge on the map!

Held annually in June.

Nashville candy maker Howell Campbell was the first confectioner to make a candy bar with multiple ingredients. Up until that time, all candy bars were solid chocolate. In 1912, Howell got the idea to combine marshmallow, peanuts, chocolate, and caramel into one little round confection, originally sold unwrapped in glass candy jars.

The bars were a big hit, becoming the company's biggest seller and the talk of the town. Delighted that his concoction was such a big hit, Howell was stumped for a name, until talking to a woman on the street. She enthused that the confection was "So good, people will ask for it from birth," reminding Howell of his son's first words. And that's the story of the Goo Goo Cluster.

TEAPOT FESTIVAL • TRENTON

The teapots this festival celebrates aren't like the teapots you'd find on a stove. Nope. These teapots are real fancy. In fact, they're not really teapots. They're veilleuse-theirres, which were made as food warmers and were used for porridge, soup, or to dispense an invalid's drink in sick rooms. They were ornamental as well as useful, with most being translucent.

The city of Trenton has the distinction of owning the World's Largest Collection of Veilleuses-Theirres. The collection, which contains 525 items, was donated by Dr. Fredrick Freed, who collected them during his international travels. They are made of the finest porcelain and date from 1750 to 1860.

The Teapot Festival was begun in 1981 to draw attention to the collection. It's grown to a week-long extravaganza, beginning with the ceremonial "Lighting of the Teapots," and culminating with a Grand Parade. In between there's a block party, music fest, a horse show, a most unusual teapot contest, a teapot lawn contest, a teapot trot, and fireworks. In between all the excitement, of course, you can tip yourself on over to the museum and view those fancy teapots that got it all started.

Held annually in April.

The aliens have landed! And, according to Brentwood resident Sandy Nichols they are four-foot tall, gray in color, with big heads and huge eyes. Oh, and there's a seven-foot version that looks the same and a lizardly lot that shows up ever now an' again.

See, Nichols is convinced that he's been abducted by aliens. More than once. In fact, it's been a regular occurrence for Nichols since he was six years old. If what he says is true, these tricky aliens consider us lowly humans the equivalent of guinea pigs. Seems they routinely beam up specimens for study, probing into our innermost thoughts...and other innermost parts!

Typically, says Nichols, the aliens wake him in the middle of the night and float him out of bed up into their UFO, which must be hovering somewhere above. They immobilize him, using their eyes in some kind of mind control. Then perform all manner of experiments on him— including, he says, the extraction of sperm. According to Nichols—and other abductees—these aliens are developing a hybrid race. They harvest human sperm and eggs for cross-fertilization. It's a fait accompli, he told a Life Magazine interviewer in 2000. He has, in fact, been shown two of his hybrid children, one that looked to be around six months and the other eighteen-years-old. Cool. At least he doesn't have to pay child support.

Strange But True Culture

Artists, world-class storytellers, music, and music men—it's culture with a twist in Strange But True Tennessee.

Artists

Folk Artists. Self-taught Artists. Outsiders. Whatever you call them, it's been said that there's just one rule in folk art: The artist must be as interesting as his art. No problem here!

HAWKINS BOLDEN

Hard times affect people differently. For some, the hard times become a hammer that beats them down. Others take that hammer and beat the hard times into art that touches the world.

Hawkins Bolden was one who didn't let the hard times get him down. Born in 1914, he was freakishly blinded as a child, when an accidental blow to the head with a baseball bat resulted in recurring seizures. During one of those seizures, Bolden's eyes became fixed on the sun, damaging the retinas and causing permanent blindness.

Blindness didn't stop Bolden from expressing himself through art—though that may not have at first been his intention. At first, he planned only to scare away the crows from his garden. He gathered discarded items from the streets around his Memphis home—hubcaps, tin coffee pots, buckets, metal baking pans, old tin cans. Beating holes into these pieces, he connected them with other found items, such as pieces of leather, wire, fabric strips, and garden hoses. To make his scarecrows scarier, he often used leather or fabric strips as protruding tongues. He then nailed the whole thing onto a piece of wood and stuck it into the soil of his garden.

Hawkins Bolden creates sculptures from found objects.
Courtesy of Negroartist.com.

Folk art collectors caught wind of his new talent, and they flocked to Bolden's garden like crows to the pecan orchard. They picked his garden clean and begged for more.

Bolden obliged gladly, using his fingers to see his materials and the creations that hid within them. "Sometimes I feel words on something, but I don't know what it is," he once said of the objects he picked up along the roadside. "I don't ask nobody about it or about color. I don't worry about color. I know when I can make something by how it feels."

Although he always called his sculptures "scarecrows," he expanded his repertoire to include life-size figures to decorate the house and yard, and smaller mask-like sculptures, with faces punched into objects, such as frying pans and metal signs. Pleased by the recognition his worked received, he worked to make them more complex, with multiple surfaces, many staring eyes, and protruding objects, all arranged on a central surface.

If the sculptures were meant to banish Bolden's demons, or if, indeed, he had any, we'll never know. He gently slipped away, passing away in his sleep on January 18, 2005.

FRANK "PREACHER" BOYLE

Like most outsider artists, Frank Boyle didn't discover his talent until later in life, a life he'd spent traveling the country. In those younger years, he worked at many famous places: The Peabody Hotel in Memphis, the Palmer House in Chicago, and the Beverly Wilshire in Los Angeles. Ah, but, he eventually found himself in Sin City. In Las Vegas, those demons, alcohol and drugs, leaped astride his back and refused to get off. He awoke one day and realized, he said, that he could either die like a dog or get his head together. He chose the latter.

Coming off the chemicals, he said he had to find a goal, and that goal was to help other substance abusers. Returning to Tennessee in 1986, he began a ministry, hence the "Preacher" nickname. He also began dabbling in art as a way to reach those substance abusers he wished to help. Bottle art is what he settled on. He painted bottles with bright patterns and face designs. We're betting it's significant that many of those bottles he's so prettily painted once held demon liquor.

Anyway, his bottles caught the eye of collectors and now he's featured in art studios across the country. Frank says his creations are a gift to him from God. If you give God the right thing, God will give it back, he says. We're grateful for Frank's gift.

SHANE CAMPBELL

Shane Campbell grew up in Tennessee, where his father was an antique dealer and a wood carver. He had always admired his father's work, and after many years of traveling the country working for a Fortune 500 company, he decided it was time to settle down. He quit his job and returned to Tennessee, where he's pursued his need to create.

He compares himself to his father, who had a "passion to work, with each carving being a form of expression—an extension of himself, his heart, his soul."

Campbell's work is whimsical, with such creations as mermaids and mermen, busty angel babes, and a black Statue of Liberty. His carvings often serve as a soap box for his peeves, such as bad drivers and big insurance companies. His work is included in the collection of the Mennello Museum in Orlando, Florida, the Santa Barbara Maritime Museum, and the American Visionary Museum.

JOHN PAUL DANIEL A.K.A. BEBO

John Paul Daniel is an untrained artist from Kingston Springs, Tennessee. Back in 1993, he had torn down an old shed behind a church and had stacked the wood, and one day, for no apparent reason, he began cutting out pieces of that wood with a hatchet. The pieces were primitive fish. A couple of months into the project, he had a dream, where someone said to him, "You are Bebo." So, he took Bebo as his folk art name.

A man of many talents, Bebo writes songs when he's not carving critters out of wood.
Courtesy of Bebo.

Bebo carves with old scrap wood. Now using a jigsaw instead of a hatchet, he carves mostly "critters," such as fish, gators, squid, lizards, and snakes of all sizes from just inches to ten feet long. The pieces are painted with tractor paint in primary colors and are usually brightly decorated.

In addition to his artwork, Daniel is a noted songwriter. His music had been recorded by such artists as Pam Tillis, Clay Walker, Sherrie Austin, and Bryan White. He says his art compliments his song writing.

Strange But True Culture

WILLIAM CROSS

William Cross's hard times started early. He was born in the Appalachian town of Erwin in 1957. His father, reportedly a real Hell's Angel of a guy, put him out at age seventeen. He became a wild mountaineer, but he kept himself fed. Still living in the mountains of Green County, his two passions are banjo playing and carving art from stone.

With no formal art training, he's been carving for twenty years, but only recently found his niche in stone (Get it, niche, stone? Ah, never mind). Collectors have discovered him and his works are appearing in collections around the country.

Of his work, Cross says, "I just see those things and I gets crazy until I get it carved in stone. Then, it takes me 15 or 16 hours to carve it with my knife and chisel in my workshop outback."

WILLIAM EDMONDSON

Considered to be a father of the American Outsider Art movement, William Edmondson was born around 1870 in the Hillsboro section of Nashville. His parents, George and Jane, were Edmondson and Compton slaves.

As a young man, Edmondson worked for the Nashville, Chattanooga, and St. Louise Railroad, and later for the Women's Hospital (now Baptist Hospital). Then the depression hit and he lost his job as an orderly at the hospital. Serendipity, it seems, for God had bigger plans for him.

One night, Edmondson said, God appeared to him in a dream and spoke to him about the talent of cutting stone that

He was about to bestow. He told him He had something for him, and instructed him to make chisels and other sculpting tools. "He talked so loud, He woke me up," he said.

Taking God at his Word, Edmondson began carving tombstones from limestone, usually from demolished buildings, for the two African-American cemeteries, Mt. Ararat and Greenwood, in Nashville. They weren't your ordinary RIP tombstones, however. They were "miracles," he said—doves, turtles, angels, horses, women, even preachers. He never lacked for materials, for his pieces were so well known that wrecking companies often would divert their trucks to his home to leave loads of limestone at no cost.

Five years after he began carving, Edmondson was discovered by the art world, when *Harper's Bazaar* photographer Louise Dahl-Wolfe brought him to the attention of Alfred Barr. As director of the Museum of Modern Art in New York, Barr was interested in "modern primitive" art, and Edmondson's carvings fit the bill precisely. He offered Edmondson the opportunity for a one-man show at the Museum of Modern Art, making him the first African-American ever accorded such an honor.

Edmondson's work soon became widely recognized and honored. His sculptures were included in the 1938 Three Centuries of Art in the United States and in 1941 he was honored with a one-man show at the Nashville Art Gallery. Because of poor health, he stopped sculpting in the mid 1940s, but recognition of his work was ongoing. He died on February 7, 1951, and was buried in Mt. Ararat.

Honors too many to enumerate were awarded posthumously to Edmondson and his work. In 1979, Nashville named a park on 17th Avenue North and Charlotte Street in his honor. A marker, appropriately carved in limestone from the Nashville's old Commerce Building, was dedicated on July 8, 1981. On it, a dove, carved by sculptor Gregory Ridley, flies above the inscription: This park is dedicated to the memory of the renowned Nashville sculptor, William Edmondson.

BESSIE HARVEY

Bessie Harvey liked to get to the root of things. One of East Tennessee's most highly acclaimed self-taught artists, Harvey created dolls using tree roots and branches, which she often gilded with glitter, beads, and strands of her own hair.

Her art reflected the difficulty of her life. Born in Dallas, Georgia, in 1929, she was forced to quit school in order her help her family survive following the death of her father. She had completed the fourth grade. Life was hard, with a regimented work schedule, washing, ironing, and cleaning for white families.

At age fourteen, she married Charles Harvey and had her first three babies. Harvey, unfortunately, was an alcoholic, and in her early twenties, Bessie left him, moving to Knoxville with her children. She worked as a housekeeper for several years before settling in Alcoa.

By age thirty-five, Harvey had eleven children and her life was an unending struggle to care for them. She later compared herself to an animal, trying to scrape together food and shelter for them. She didn't become human, she said, until her youngest was half-grown.

It wasn't until she was in her forties that Harvey began making art. In despair over the death of her mother, she found strength in her faith. God, she said, had shown her how to find the spiritual presence living in gnarled tree roots, branches, and stumps. She brought her root figures, animals, and masks to life with paint, and adorned them with found objects, such as feathers, jewels, beads, shells, and even her own hair.

Her works often told Bible tales and reflected her feelings about the continuous struggle against racism, the strife of poverty, and personal hardship. As her work became known, its otherwordly quality inspired collectors to speculate that her style had its origins in African voodoo, which hurt and angered Harvey because of her devout Christianity. The charge did, however, spawn an interest in African art.

Harvey's magical ability to evoke characters from gnarled roots propelled her to the forefront of American Folk art. In 1995, a year after her death, her work was selected for inclusion in the Whitney Museum of American Art's 1995 Biennial. Additionally, her work has been included in practically every African-American show since 1990.

DANNY "THE BUCKET MAN" HOSKINSON

No doubt about it, Danny Hoskinson has recycling down to an art. It all started back in 1987 at a July 4 picnic at Lake Lanier. Hoskinson discovered a unique talent. Using a butane lighter, he began wowing his friends with his ability to melt plastic forks and spoons into a variety of shapes and sculptures. That event sparked the idea to increase the size of his sculptures.

At his studio in Benton, Hoskins now uses a blowtorch to melt down five-

Danny "The Bucket Man" Hoskinson molds sculptures from melted plastic.
Courtesy of Orange Hill.

gallon plastic buckets—most of which are donated by local restaurants. The buckets melt into a clay-like substance Hoskinson molds into fanciful and mystical figures, borne of a unique imagination. You'll find alligators with swiveling heads, two-headed turtles, and swimming cows. Some of his figures are half human, half…something else. There are also totem poles, birds, horses, aliens, alligators, and snakes.

As you can tell from his artwork, Hoskinson is a colorful character who, as a house painter, was known as the barefoot painter, because he was always shoeless. A self-proclaimed free spirit, he says, "While working, I like to think that I am teaching the plastic to be art and the plastic is teaching me to be the artist."

DOW PUGH

Dow Pugh was born in Monterey, Tennessee, in 1906. He was sixteen when he left to find work, and he didn't return until his wife and son were killed in an accident thirty-five years later. He restored his mother's Cumberland Mountain log cabin and moved in. Living alone, he found himself incapable of sitting without a knife and a piece of wood to whittle on.

He began by carving busts of famous people, but then became known as the Indian, Snake, and Gourd Man, for the Indian artifacts he collected and his artwork that included heads made from gourds. He decorated the outside of the cabin with wall sculptures, paintings, and life-size figures. Inside was an eclectic collection of Civil War hats, old golf caps, World War I helmets, musical instruments, snake skins, and carved masks.

Pugh died in 1993 but his work lives on. The Museum of Appalachia in Norris has a permanent display of his work and pieces can be found for sale at America Oh Yes! Gallery.

VANNOY "WIREMAN" STREETER

When folks said Vannoy Streeter was wired, they didn't mean he carried his Nextel on his hip. Naw. They meant he sure knows how to twist wire into art. Streeter first became known for his stylized wire sculptures of Tennessee Walking Horses. He had gained a lifelong fascination for the breed when he worked as a stable boy for Strolling Jim, the first grand champion Walking horse.

By the mid-1980s, television and print features about Streeter brought regional attention to his work, that drew heavily on childhood influences. Folk art collectors began flocking to his home. His fame soon became widespread, through showings at galleries, exhibits, and shops. In 1990, he was a demonstrating artist at the National Black Arts Festival and was honored as the Heritage Craftsman for 1991.

Despite the recognition, Streeter was modest about his work. He'd often give it away, telling the person to keep it, because after all, "It's just a piece of wire." He presented several musicians, including Jimmy Buffett, Paul Simon, Mary Chapin Carpenter, and the Smashing Pumpkins, with "Smitty" sculptures.

Today, Streeter's work is displayed in exhibits around the world, and most recently was featured at the White House and the U.S. Embassy in Beijing. Streeter died on May 13, 1999.

E.T. WICKHAM

Enoch T. Wickham was born in 1883 in Palmyra. A farmer with nine children, he began making concrete sculptures in the 1950s. He was a self-taught artist, who made his life-size sculptures using pipes and wire as re-enforcement. He used stove pipes as molds for making the pillars to his monuments.

His statues immortalized such historic figures as Patrick Henry, Andrew Jackson, General William Westmoreland, John and Robert Kennedy, Estes Kefauver, Tecumseh, and Sergeant York. Some of the subjects of Wickham's figures, such as General Westmoreland and Estes Kefauver, attended the dedication ceremonies of their statues. In all, he made forty statues and placed them on his land in Palmyra.

Unfortunately, after his death in 1970, the statues remained where he had left them, unguarded and uncared for. Weather and vandals have taken a toll on them, and some are now headless or armless. In recent years, Wickham's grandson, Joe Schibig, has made an effort to preserve the remaining statues and bring attention to them and his grandfather's legacy. A few have been moved to a place of safety at Austin Peay State University in Clarksville. Shibig hopes to have a park established at the Palmyra site.

Music From The Heart

Oh, Lauzy Mercy. Just where do we start? Tennessee is all about music. You can't avoid it. It's everywhere you turn; in every step you take; floating to you over the mountains and the valleys.

ROY ACUFF

Roy Acuff, born in 1903 in Maynardsville, had dreams of becoming a great baseball player. He made it to the minor leagues, but an injury ended his career. Baseball's loss was music's gain. Disappointed, he began learning to play his father's fiddle, and was soon playing in a traveling medicine show.

In 1934, Acuff and his band began auditioning to play for the popular radio shows, WROL and WNOX in Knoxville and the WSM's *Grand Ole Opry*. They played on WROL and WNOX, where they gained a following and a WROL announcer dubbed the band the Crazy Tennesseans. They were repeatedly turned down for the *Opry*, however.

From their WROL performances, they caught the attention of a Chicago recording company, and were given the opportunity to record twenty songs. The band began experimenting with the day's popular crooning styles mixed with traditional sounds, but Acuff was partial to the hillbilly music he grew up with in his Cumberland Mountain home.

Finally, given the opportunity to play the *Opry*, the band performed the classic "The Great Speckled Bird" in that new fangled crooning style. The audience reception was lukewarm and not many fan letters were written. When they were asked back for a return engagement, they again played "The Great Speckled Bird," only this time they went hillbilly all the way. The song was an instant hit, and Acuff and the band, renamed the Smoky Mountain Boys, soon joined the *Opry* as featured artists.

Acuff's next recording, "The Wabash Cannonball," was a big hit, and Opry executives put the singer at the center of their budding star system. His popularity exploded, and as it grew, he helped to solidify the *Grand Old Opry* and WSM as the center of country music.

During the 1930s and 1940s, Acuff sold more records than any other country singer, and was one of the first ever country music stars. His show was one of the first complete stage shows, including vaudeville/minstrel-style skits and slapstick comedy.

Acuff remained active in the country music field throughout his life, recording for several labels, touring constantly, appearing on the television show *Hee Haw*, and playing on the *Grand Ole Opry*. He also ran, unsuccessfully, for governor of

Tennessee—twice. In 1962, he was inducted into the Country Music Hall of Fame, the first ever living member. Acuff died on November 23, 1992.

CHARLIE BOWMAN

Fiddlin' Charlie Bowman was known as the "champion fiddler of East Tennessee." The son of an old-time fiddler, Bowman first learned to play a homemade banjo at age twelve. Not long after, he picked up an old fiddle and began sawing away. This, he decided, was the instrument for him. He went out and bought a fiddle for $4.50, which he once said was the best fiddle he ever had.

Bowman's four brothers each played a different musical instrument, and before long, the brothers were entertaining at local functions, sometimes being paid around 75 cents each. But mostly they played for what they could get passing the hat— and some nights they were lucky to get the hat back.

In the early 1920s, a friend of Bowman's, who'd heard him play, gave him $5 to enter a fiddling contest in Johnson City. Bowman didn't figure he had much of a chance, seeing as the Georgia champion fiddler was going to be there, but, hey it was five bucks. He won second place, and was paid $25 more. Well, sir, here was an idée!

Fiddlin' Charlie began entering fiddler's contests all around the Southeast, and he was winning them. Won so many, in fact, that people began to complain, thinking maybe the judges were playin' favorites. So, at the next contest, the judges were placed where they couldn't see the contestants. Bowman still won.

Bowman was playing with his brothers, and they became well known around East Tennessee for a while. He went on to play and record with a band called the Hill Billies, with whom he played at the White House for President Calvin Coolidge. Bowman also penned the songs "East Tennessee Blues," "Nine Pound Hammer," and "Roll On Buddy."

After the Hill Billies, he joined the Blue Ridge Ramblers for a while, then formed his own band. He was quick with an ad lib and enjoyed writing and performing comedy skits along with his music. In addition to the fiddle, he was proficient in fifteen standard instruments and quite a few substandard ones, including brooms, saws, washtubs, and balloons.

In 1957, Bowman stopped performing. He remained involved with old time music, however, enjoying a brief revival in 1960. He died in 1962 at age seventy-two.

> Nashville has more than eighty record labels, one hundred and thirty music publishers, one hundred and eighty recording studios, and five thousand union musicians. No wonder it is internationally known as the Music City.

Lester Flatt

Lester Flatt was a pioneer in bluegrass music. Ranking as a preeminent guitar player and singer, he is credited with helping to make Bluegrass what it is today.

A good ol' Tennessee boy, born in Sparta in 1914, Flatt started out working in the textile mills. But the music of his fathers echoed in his ears, and by the 1940s, he'd picked up his guitar and started picking on stage.

In 1945, he joined Bill Monroe's Blue Grass Boys, where he became a part of the band that fathered bluegrass music, which was named for his band. Flatt, along with banjo player Earl Scruggs and other band members, played a pivotal role in its development. With Bill Monroe's high tenor vocals and hot mandolin playing, Flatt's lead singing and warm guitar, and Scruggs's banjo playing (using the distinctive "three finger roll" he perfected and that became a distinguishing characteristic of bluegrass), they rocked the music world with their novel sound.

Flatt and Scruggs left the band in 1948 and formed their own band, The Foggy Mountain Boys, where for twenty-one years they continued to define Bluegrass music. In 1953, Martha White Flour began sponsoring Flatt & Scruggs in daily radio shows on WSM and continued to support them for the rest of their career. In 1955, they joined the Grand Ole Opry and enjoyed success on the country charts with their recordings. Appearances at the Norfolk Folk Festival and on national TV brought national acclaim, and paved the way for a series of folk albums.

Their fame brought them to the attention of a Hollywood producer with a new show in the works. Flatt and Scruggs, Ash Grove thought, were perfect to sing the show's opening song. The duo wrote the theme to *The Beverly Hillbillies*, the most popular TV series in history, and the group played and sang it. It quickly hit the top of the charts, their only number one hit. They also appeared on the show frequently as themselves.

Business and musical differences caused Flatt and Scruggs to part ways. Both men continued to perform for many years afterward. Flatt reassembled the Foggy Mountain Boys, renamed them the Nashville Grass and, keeping to his traditional bluegrass roots, toured successfully until his death in 1979. Flatt and Scruggs were inducted into the Country Music Hall of Fame in 1985.

"TENNESSEE" ERNIE FORD

It's hard to decide what Ernie Ford is best known for. Certainly his gargantuan international hit "Sixteen Tons" is at the top of the list. But then, there's also his prime time TV shows in the 1960s, where his expression "Bless your little pea pickin' heart," became a national catch phrase. And his extensive run of Top 10 country-come-pop hits. And the phenomenal number of gospel hits he recorded.

Ford's fifty-year legacy is astounding. Over the years, he sold more than 60 million records worldwide, more than 40 million of which were gospel, hymns, and spirituals. His musical and performing achievements won him three stars on the Hollywood Walk of Fame—for Radio, Music, and Television. He was a Grammy winner in 1964 for his album *Great Gospel Songs*. He was a recipient of the Minnie Pearl Award for his contributions to country and pop music. In 1990, he was inducted into the Country Music Hall of Fame.

On October 8, 1984, then-President Ronald Reagan bestowed on Ford the Presidential Medal, the highest honor a president can award a civilian. In his one-page citation, Reagan summed up

Ford's legacy best: "America is a nation richer in spirit because of Tennessee Ernie Ford."

The old pea picker picked his last pea on October 17, 1991.

"Tennessee" Ernie Ford circa 1945 at WOPI, Bristol, Tennessee.
Courtesy of William H. Mountjoy Jr.

ARETHA FRANKLIN

Lady Soul was born in Memphis on March 25, 1942. Best known for her number one hit "Respect," Aretha Franklin is a gospel, soul, and R&B singer who is regarded as one of the best vocalists ever.

Although she's had only two number one hits, Franklin has won seventeen Grammys, of which an unprecedented eleven were for Best Female R&B Vocal Performance. In 1987, she became the first woman to be inducted into the Rock and Roll Hall of Fame. The state of Michigan, where she grew up, has declared her voice a natural wonder.

THE GRAND OLE OPRY

The Grand Ole Opry started out in 1925 as the *WSM Barn Dance*, broadcast from the radio's new studio in the National Life & Accident Insurance Company in Nashville. The show's

first performer was eighty-year-old fiddler, Uncle Jimmy
Thompson. Conceived and produced by George Hay, who,
though just thirty, called himself the Solemn Old Judge, the
show was called the *WSM Barn Dance* until 1926. It was
renamed by a chance remark. Seems the show followed NBC
Radio Network's *Music Appreciation Hour*, a presentation of
classical music. When the *WSM Barn Dance* came on, Hay
remarked that after an hour of Grand Opera, they'd now be
presenting the *Grand Ole Opry*.

In the 1930s, popular recording artist Roy Acuff began
appearing regularly on the *Opry*. He's credited with giving the
show credibility and centering country music in Nashville. The
small studio of the National Life and Accident Company
quickly became too small for the crowds of people flocking to
each performance. The show moved several times before
settling into the
Ryman
Auditorium in
1943, where it
stayed until 1974.

The *Grand Ole
Opry* was and still
is one of the
most influential
vehicles for
stardom in
country music.
Hundreds of

June Carter Cash performs at *The Grand Ole Opry*.
Courtesy Larry D. Moore.

performers have entertained on its stage, from new stars to superstars to legends. Today, little kids who grew up listening to the *Opry* in darkened bedrooms across the country are now the stars of the stage, names such as Reba McEntire, Vince Gill, Alan Jackson, and Garth Brooks.

Today, country music is the most listened to music in the country and the *Grand Ole Opry*, as the longest continuously running radio program in the world, is still doing its part to bring country music to the world. Located in the 4,400-seat Grand Ole Opry House just outside of Nashville, the Opry is broadcast to radio stations around the world. It's shown frequently on PBS, and is a weekly presentation on the cable network channel Great American Country, where a new generation of future stars is listening.

Although the *Grand Old Opry* moved to a new stage in 1974, today's singers can still be awed at playing on the same stage as country music greats—and firsts—Dave Macon, Hank Williams, Patsy Cline, Ernest Tubb, and others. That's because when the *Opry* moved into its new home at the Grand Ole Opry House, a six foot circle of the Ryman Auditorium stage was cut out and installed on the new stage. Huh. Let's all sing now...May the circle be unbroken...

Strange But True Culture

UNCLE DAVE MACON

Dave Macon, nicknamed the Dixie Dewdrop by George Hay, was the *Grand Ole Opry*'s first star. Born in the 1870 in Smartt, he was one of the most colorful personalities in country music history. He was an influential bridge between the folk and vaudeville music of the nineteenth century and the modern music introduced by the phonograph, radio, and movies.

Macon didn't begin his musical career until the age of fifty, spurred mostly by the fact that motorized trucks had put his mule delivery company out of business. He was an extremely skilled banjo picker, with more than nineteen different picking styles.

In addition, he was an outrageous comedian and his shows always featured skits and routines that had audiences slapping their knees and rolling in the aisles with laughter.

Macon recorded more than 180 songs for most every major label from 1924 until 1938. Historians consider his songs priceless, both for the variety of banjo styles they preserve and the look back they give into the songs of the nineteenth century.

One of the two charter members of the WSM Barn Dance, Macon appeared on the *Grand Ole Opry* until his death in 1952 when he was eighty-something. He was inducted into the Country Music Hall of Fame in 1966.

Writers

Tennessee also has its share of notable writers too. Here are a couple you may recognize.

JAMES AGEE

Novelist, journalist, screenwriter, poet, and film critic, James Agee was a well rounded writer. He was born at 15th and Highland Streets, and when his father was killed in a car crash when he was six, Agee was sent to a boarding school for boys. He attended Saint Andrew's School for Mountain Boys, now Saint Andrews-Sewannee School and was in the 1928 class of Phillips Exeter Academy, one of the nation's leading boarding high school located in New Hampshire, where he edited the *Monthly*. He then attended Harvard, where he was president of the Harvard Advocate. He graduated in 1932.

His early years included stints at *Fortune* magazine and , and then at *Time*.

Agee's first book of poetry, *Permit Me Voyage*, was published in 1938 and in 1941, he published a book from material gathered in Alabama titled *Let Us Now Praise Famous Men*. The book sold only six hundred copies. In 1942, he became the film critic for *Time* magazine and later became quite influential as the film critic for *The Nation* magazine. In 1948, he quit to freelance, writing magazine articles and book reviews and working as a scriptwriter, where he wrote the screenplay for *The African Queen*.

It's a shame to say, but sometimes, a fella has to die for folks to take notice of his work. Throughout his adult life, Agee had worked on an autobiographical book, which examined the effect of his father's death on his family. Though the book was incomplete, a friend edited it and it was published in 1957 under the title *A Death in the Family*. The book won the 1958 Pulitzer Prize for Fiction. Additionally, his book *Let Us Now Praise Famous Men* was rediscovered and is now celebrated as an important portrait of 1930's America.

ALEX HALEY

For many of us Southerners, Alex Haley is Kunta Kinte. In the made-for-TV movie based on Haley's book *Roots*, first aired in 1977, the appalling capture of this noble African and his fight to hold onto the traditions of his homeland amid the indignities he faced as a slave in the South, served as an education to the unenlightened.

The movie caused a sensation. While many viewers found no revelation, many others saw horror in the story and felt shame at sharing ancestry with people who had the audacity to consider themselves superior.

Ah, but Alex Haley is more than the sum of his *Roots*. Born in New York, but raised in Henning, he joined the Coast Guard, where he began his writing career, penning love letters for his fellow sailors to send to their wives and girlfriends. He also submitted other writings to magazines, but racked up rejection slip after rejection slip, eight years' worth before selling his first piece.

After twenty years of service, he left the National Guard to become a full-time writer, writing biographical features for the

Reader's Digest. In 1965, he produced *The Autobiography of Malcom X*. It was his first major work and had immense effects on the black power movement in the U.S.

Roots, published in 1976, was next. It gained critical and popular success and garnered Haley the National Book Award and a special Pulitzer Prize. Haley also wrote a history of Henning, various short stories, and the epic novel *Queen*, and collaborated with producer Norman Lear on the TV series *Palmersdale, U.S.A.*, which was based on his boyhood experiences in Henning.

Haley died of a heart attack on February 10, 1992.